MW00930971

Workbook for The Body Keeps the Score

Practical Steps for Healing

Dr. Kael Lifeson

© Copyright 2023 - All rights reserved.

The content contained within this book may not be reproduced, duplicated or transmitted without direct written permission from the author or the publisher.

Under no circumstances will any blame or legal responsibility be held against the publisher, or author, for any damages, reparation, or monetary loss due to the information contained within this book, either directly or indirectly.

Legal Notice:

This book is copyright protected. It is only for personal use. You cannot amend, distribute, sell, use, quote or paraphrase any part, or the content within this book, without the consent of the author or publisher.

Disclaimer Notice:

Please note the information contained within this document is for educational and entertainment purposes only. All effort has been executed to present accurate, up to date, reliable, complete information. No warranties of any kind are declared or implied. Readers acknowledge that the author is not engaged in the rendering of legal, financial, medical or professional advice. The content within this book has been derived from various sources. Please consult a licensed professional before attempting any techniques outlined in this book.

By reading this document, the reader agrees that under no circumstances is the author responsible for any losses, direct or indirect, that are incurred as a result of the use of the information contained within this document, including, but not limited to, errors, omissions, or inaccuracies.

Table of Contents

INTRODUCTION

One of the main tasks of life is to learn how to care for ourselves and how to open our hearts to those we love.

Taking care of ourselves well requires attention, while some things we do automatically. We do not need to be reminded to adjust our pH level, we do that by breathing. Some information, like painful joints when you are overweight, the inability to know what your desires are, or feeling so numb that beauty does not excite you, needs our attention. Our symptoms, in a sense, provide us feedback if we can listen to them. We might not listen, and instead, we may ignore them, explain them away, or medicate them into silence. *The Body Keeps the Score*, written by Dr. Bessel van der Kolk, will help us "read" the symptoms of trauma.

The Body Keeps the Score has been widely praised as a modern classic in the psychiatric literature on trauma, and hailed as a major breakthrough in treating one of the most crippling experiences of human life. However, it is a long and difficult book to read. For those who don't have the time or the energy, then this is the book for you. Here, we have a summary of the theory and practice found in *The Body Keeps the Score*.

What is trauma? Why is it important?

As Dr. Bessel van der Kolk (2014) describes:

Nobody can "treat" a war, or abuse, rape, molestation, or any other horrendous event, for that matter; what has happened cannot be undone. But what can be dealt with are the imprints of the trauma on body, mind, and soul: the crushing sensations in your chest that you may label as anxiety or depression; the fear of losing control; always being on alert for danger or rejection; the self-loathing; the nightmares and flashbacks; the fog that keeps you from staying on task and from engaging fully in what you are doing; being unable to fully open your heart to another human being. (p.1)

Dr. Bessel van der Kolk notes that trauma is an injury, not a disease. For Van der Kolk, trauma happens because a terrible event, or a series of events, overwhelms the central nervous system. It leaves a person feeling like they are no longer at home in their body. It is a state the other researchers call ontological insecurity. Trauma, in biological terms, changes our nervous system. Our perception of what safety is, and what a threat is, changes too.

Trauma is not limited to soldiers on the battlefield or those living in war-torn regions. It can affect anyone: ourselves and our loved ones. In the United States, research over the last decade has pointed to trauma experienced at home rather than lands far away. One in five Americans experienced some form of sexual abuse in childhood, one in favor have been physically abused by a parent, and one in three experience domestic violence. These findings, from the Centers for Disease Control and Prevention, are harrowing. Additionally, a quarter of people in Western societies have grown up with alcoholic family members, and one in eight have witnessed their mother being physically abused. This is only likely to have gotten worse post-pandemic. However, there is some good news, and we can give you two pieces.

First, human beings are resilient as a species. We have endured wars, famine, natural disasters, pandemics, and personal betrayals throughout history. The bad news is that these can leave "traces" that affect our immune system, our ability to experience intimacy, and even our capacity for joy. In other words, after a traumatic experience has ended, the part of our brain responsible for our survival remains responsive to the slightest hint of danger. We change from being gardeners to the general of an army. This can reactivate a trauma and trigger intense physical and emotional responses, disturbing sensations, impulsive behavior, aggression and despair. People feel like they are no longer in control and are beyond repair.

Treating trauma has historically focused on the psychological effects, relying on insight, whereas Dr. Van der Kolk's book helps us ignore what seems to be the most obvious thing, and this is the second piece of good news. Van der Kolk draws our attention to the effects that trauma has on the body (and without ignoring the mind).

The book provides a comprehensive understanding of trauma through a combination of engaging narratives, accessible explanations of neurobiology, and insightful critiques of traditional treatment methods. It introduces innovative approaches that help patients heal beyond their conscious minds by addressing the frozen parts of their past, and illustrates these approaches with vivid case histories alongside compelling research. However, few of us can read the whole book.

The Avenues of Healing Trauma and the Structure of the Workbook

According to van der Kolk, there are three primary avenues of healing. The first involves talking about it. Here, we are giving language to our experience, a "coming to terms" with what happened, and thereby processing the memory. The second involves taking medication that can shut down inappropriate alarm systems, while the third is by helping the body have experiences that deeply and viscerally contradict helplessness, rage, or the collapse that result from trauma. From these three avenues, *The Body Keeps the Score* recommends six practices that a person can use to heal from trauma.

1) **Mindfulness practices:** Van der Kolk suggests practicing mindfulness exercises, such as yoga and meditation, to help regulate the nervous system and reduce anxiety and stress. We focus on these in Chapter 1.

2) **Physical exercise:** Regular physical exercise can help to release tension and stress stored in the body, promote the production of feel-good chemicals like endorphins, and improve overall well-being. This is the focus of Chapter 2.

3) **Eye movement desensitization and reprocessing (EMDR):** This therapy uses rapid eye movements to help process traumatic memories and reduce their emotional impact. We will discuss different kinds of therapy in Chapter 5.

4) **Neurofeedback:** This therapy uses real-time displays of brain activity to help individuals learn to regulate their nervous system and manage symptoms of trauma. Since we are unlikely to have the right technology at home, this won't be covered in the book.

5) **Somatic experiencing:** This therapy involves working with bodily sensations to help individuals process traumatic experiences and release stored emotions. Breathwork is an important tool here, as well as trauma and tension release exercises, which are taken up in Chapter 2.

6) **Creative expression:** Van der Kolk suggests that engaging in creative activities, such as art, music, and dance, can help individuals express their emotions and promote healing. This is the focus of Chapter 3.

In this workbook, we are not going to focus on Van der Kolk's experiments, research findings, scholarly references, literature reviews, and patient vignettes to support the validity of different treatments. All the extra information has been distilled into exercises a person can do to heal at home, with others, or by themselves, for free.

Each chapter has a focus, which begins with some theory and ends with a practical step-by-step beginner's guide just to get you going.

What Is the Essential Message of This Book?

Each chapter will outline practical exercises, buttressed by the basic idea of why they are important, to reactivate this system. Each chapter focuses on a different part of ourselves as human beings, to instill the hope that, after trauma, we can piece ourselves back together again.

These exercises also complement each other. It means if one exercise falls away, while others are maintained, you can come back to it easily. There may be a season for specific exercises, and a season for others, there is no need to do it perfectly. They are adaptable to our own situations and preferences. Find the rhythm that works for you, and then improve on it; see what sparks joy, and follow that. Or, you might want to focus on something specific, and turn to the other exercises when you need them. Dabble and experiment!

A key theme in research on trauma is that trauma fractures interdependent elements in a given system. In other words, relationships. Looking beyond the specific symptoms that are used to diagnose mental illness, we see that almost all mental suffering is related to difficulties in either **creating fulfilling relationships** or **regulating arousal**, such as becoming overly angry, shutting down, overexcited, or disorganized. Typically, it's a combination. Hence, the exercises in the book, except for Chapter 1, focus on **communal** exercises: exercises that offer the chance to be in a relationship with others.

The conventional medical approach is to simply find the right medication to treat a particular disorder. Of course, this can be helpful, because it can help us regulate our arousal. However, it can distract us from addressing how our problems affect our ability to function as members of our community. If trauma fragments our connection with the mind, our connection with our body, our connections with our senses, and connection with our loved ones, then we heal by restoring the connection.

Chapter 1

THE MIND

The Effects of Trauma on the Mind

General Effects on the Mind

Bessel van der Kolk, after decades of research, explains that trauma can have a profound impact on how the mind functions and how people experience the world around them. This chapter offers practical ways to connect with the mind, based on the findings of *The Body Keeps the Score*, as well as my personal experience while working as a therapist.

One of the main points that Van der Kolk makes is that trauma can disrupt the brain's normal functioning, particularly in areas related to emotion regulation and self-awareness. When a person experiences trauma, their brain can become stuck in a state of hyperarousal, constantly on high alert for potential threats. This can lead to symptoms such as anxiety, panic attacks, and hypervigilance, as well as physical symptoms such as rapid heart rate and sweating. We need to find ways where we are better able to regulate our emotions, and foster feelings of calm, compassion, pleasure, and relaxation.

Another way that trauma can affect the mind is by disrupting memory processing. Van der Kolk explains that traumatic memories are often stored in a different part of the brain than non-traumatic memories, which can make them more difficult to access and integrate into a person's overall sense of self. This can lead to symptoms such as flashbacks and nightmares, as well as a sense of detachment from one's own experiences. We need to feel safe if we are to access those memories.

The Mohawk of Self-Awareness

When you don't have anything specific in your mind, it turns out that your brain activates different areas that work together to create a sense of self. This includes the midline structures of the brain (on a neuroimage, it looks like a Mohawk, hence it is called the Mohawk of self-awareness). These structures are located right above our eyes and run through the center of the brain all the way to the back. When scientists scanned normal subjects, these areas activated normally. It also turns out that these are connected to brain areas that register sensations from the rest of the body.

Interestingly, the scans of eighteen chronic PTSD patients showed no activation of the self-sensing areas of the brain. The only area that showed up was the area needed for the basic orientation of space. The contrast with healthy individuals is startling.

There could only be one explanation: after experiencing prolonged terror, the only way to cope was to "cut-off" their connection to those visceral feelings and emotions. Yet, in everyday life, those same brain areas are responsible for registering the entire range of emotions and sensations that form the foundation of self-awareness. This is a tragic adaptation: in an effort to shut off a terrifying sensation, a person's capacity to be fully alive is deadened too.

The loss of this area of activation in the medial prefrontal cortex clarifies why individuals who've experienced trauma lack a sense of direction and purpose. They couldn't comprehend what they wanted. More precisely, their bodily sensations were attempting to convey messages. If they couldn't "read" them, then how could they carry out their own plans for their lives?

The implication, therefore, is clear: to feel present you have to know where you are and be aware of what is going on with you. We need to find ways to re-activate the self-sensing system once it breaks down. This is why connecting to our minds is absolutely essential.

There are other problems that are taken up in later chapters. Van der Kolk notes that trauma can disrupt the development of self-awareness and self-esteem, leading to feelings of shame, guilt, and worthlessness. Trauma can also make it difficult for people to form and maintain close relationships, as they may struggle with trust and intimacy. In addition to these cognitive and emotional effects, trauma can also have physical effects on the brain and body. Van der Kolk explains that trauma can cause changes in the brain's stress response system, leading to increased inflammation and a heightened risk for chronic health problems such as heart disease, autoimmune disorders, chronic pain, and digestive problems.

While all this information might be quite a lot to take in, I've boiled down the essentials below, and included practical steps to heal our minds.

The Garden of Our Mind

Meditation is complex, and to understand what we do when we meditate, we can think of the mind as a garden. Every garden needs space, sunshine, air, soil, and water to be healthy. However, the garden might not be able to naturally access all of those resources at the right time. This chapter includes four practices of mind, each relating to these fundamental elements: a space to meditate, mindfulness (air), koans (water), delight (sunshine), and compassion (soil).

To connect with our minds, we meditate. Good thoughts, stories, dreams, and fantasies are the sign of a healthy mind, things that allow us to live with hope, courage, honesty, kindness, and mercy. Like plants in a healthy garden, they can bloom and offer sustenance, the fruits of compassion, delight, koans, and mindfulness. The mind is not a single, static thing, but a living entity that is shaped and cultivated over time. We can be fed by our minds, or at their mercy.

A mind that has been traumatized is not a garden struck by a natural disaster. This is a part of life. A storm can uproot trees, destroy plants, and wash away soil. There is real loss, but that is not to be dismayed: a garden can be restored, reshaped, and revitalized if there is a skilled gardener available. This is true with our experience of grief, rage, depression, bereavement, despair, and so on, as parts of life. Difficult experiences can disrupt a person's psycho-emotional landscape, but that might make space for new growth if the gardener is wise.

Trauma is different. When we are traumatized, we are no longer a gardener after a natural disaster, but the general of an army. Generals are hyper-vigilant and their attention is not focused on a garden, it is focused on danger and security. They will neglect to grow a garden and re-prioritise resources towards safety or aggression to ward off threats. Of course, being the general of an army is useful when we are under attack. But what if we are safe again? And what do army generals know about gardening? Once a garden is neglected after a natural disaster, there is no possibility for renewal. This changes the way we pay attention.

When someone is traumatized, it is difficult to be aware and connected to the present moment. It creates a kind of attention that is constantly distracted by anything that signals danger, real or otherwise. Even when someone is safe in the present moment, they feel anxious, as though under threat, like the general of an army, or a politician who has an assassin after them. It is a mind that is disconnected from the present and trapped by events in the past and worries about the future. To make our garden healthy again, the first step is to build a shrine.

Space: Building a Meditation Garden

Bessel van der Kolk does not directly speak about building a meditation "garden", since it may be called a shrine which has religious connotations. There is no need for a shrine to be a religious symbol. It can be another word for your "garden". Building a shrine at home can be a meaningful and personal way to create a space for meditation. One does not have to be religious, or belong to a certain culture, to create a shrine or appreciate it. One simply needs a space to come back to in order to meditate, where, like a gardener, one comes to cultivate their spiritual life or the health of their mind.

The steps to build a shrine or meditation garden are as follows: (1) choose a location, (2) choose the right objects, (3) arrange them mindfully, (4) practice.

Preferably, choose a location that is private. It could be the corner of a room. It may also be useful to give it a theme, which may be helpful to decide which objects to include as part of the shrine. For instance, if you want to create a shrine focused on a particular spiritual tradition or teacher, or you may choose to create a shrine that reflects your own personal beliefs and values. It might also be the faces of people who love you, or other kinds of symbols that remind you of wisdom, beauty, and joy. Some common objects that people include in their shrine include:

- A statue or image of a spiritual figure or figures.

- A candle or oil lamp to represent the light of wisdom.

- Incense or essential oils to create a soothing and relaxing atmosphere.

- A small bowl of water to symbolize purity and clarity of mind.

- Crystals or gemstones to enhance energy and focus.

- Sacred texts or books that inspire you.

- Offerings of food, flowers, or other items that hold special meaning for you.

Once you have chosen the objects for your shrine, arrange them in a way that feels aesthetically pleasing and meaningful to you. You may want to use a tablecloth or other decorative cloth to create an altar space, and you might also want to add other details.

Once your shrine is complete, take time to sit and meditate in front of it regularly. Make it a ritual: Use your shrine as a place for reflection, meditation, or prayer. Set aside time each day or week to sit in front of your shrine and connect with the items you've chosen. Light candles or incense, offer prayers or affirmations, and allow yourself to fully immerse in the healing energy of your space.

It is very important to make it a ritual, since trauma makes our minds very disorganized. We need to structure the time of our day, not like a general, but like a musician: we give it a rhythm. Use your shrine as a place for reflection, meditation, or prayer. Set aside time each day or week to sit in front of your shrine and connect with the items you've chosen. Light candles or incense, offer prayers or affirmations, and allow yourself to fully immerse in the healing energy of your space.

As you continue to heal and grow, your needs and interests may change. Allow your shrine to evolve with you by adding or removing items as needed. Be open to new symbols and experiences that resonate with you, and allow your shrine to be a reflection of your ongoing journey. Of course, this can be a powerful way to connect with your spiritual practice and deepen your sense of inner peace and clarity.

However, it is difficult to know how to practice well. I will offer some guidelines for the next part of the chapter. These are not meant to be rules, but just to offer a direction where having none at all might be confusing, especially since there are a number of ways to practice meditation. Here, we will emphasize essential practices of meditation to keep the garden of your mind healthy.

Air: Mindfulness

Dr. Bessel van der Kolk believes that mindfulness helps to heal trauma by bringing awareness to the present moment. Mindfulness can help individuals who have experienced trauma by teaching them to become more aware and accepting of their present-moment experiences. By learning to be more present and less reactive to their thoughts and emotions, individuals can begin to reprocess their traumatic experiences as belonging to their past rather than their present. It is also the bedrock of connecting with our bodies, so we can begin to notice the ways we do (or do not) regulate, relax, or stress out.

The Benefits of Mindfulness

It is pretty hard to sell the idea that sitting down, closing your eyes, and breathing consistently can have remarkable benefits. With that in mind, here are some of the findings from the scientific research in the area which will hopefully convince you.

1. **Increase body awareness:** Trauma can cause individuals to disconnect from their bodies, leading to symptoms such as dissociation and numbing. Mindfulness can help individuals reconnect with their bodies and increase awareness of bodily sensations.

2. **Improve emotional regulation:** Trauma can lead to intense and overwhelming emotions. Mindfulness can help individuals regulate their emotions by teaching them to observe their emotions without judgment or reactivity.

3. **Enhance cognitive flexibility:** Trauma can lead to rigid thinking patterns and a sense of being stuck in the past. Mindfulness can help individuals develop greater cognitive flexibility, allowing them to shift their focus to the present moment and develop new perspectives.

4. **Foster self-compassion:** Trauma can cause individuals to blame themselves and feel shame for their experiences. Mindfulness can help individuals develop self-compassion, by teaching them to be kind and understanding towards themselves and their experiences.

All of these benefits essentially stem from non-judgment, which I am going to spend more time talking about because it is complicated and important. If mindfulness means to pay attention to our experience as it unfolds, which improves our bodily awareness, emotional regulation, and cognitive flexibility, and fosters self-compassion, then it opens us to a greater connection with life as it is.

When we are traumatized, our rigid alarm systems may make us blind us to what else the experience could mean. We may only see the palm of a hand, a palm that can slap us, and ignore that it has a back with knuckles, hair, wrinkles, and tendons that grant it the ability to share and to hold, not only to slap. It is the same with something like grief: grief can be seen only as pain, and something to avoid or medicate. However, since it is the other side of love, it is also the highest form of praise. Yet, we may judge the palm only for its capacity to hurt, and not its capacity to hold. This is how judgment can be harmful rather than discerning.

When we judge our experiences, we are essentially imposing values and beliefs onto the present moment. We may label certain experiences as "good" or "bad", "pleasant" or "unpleasant", based on our own biases and preferences. This can create a sense of resistance or aversion to certain experiences, which can ultimately lead to more suffering. Hence, cognitive flexibility is enormously helpful.

When we approach our experiences with a non-judgmental attitude, we are able to cultivate a greater sense of equanimity and acceptance. We are able to respond to our experiences with greater clarity and wisdom, rather than reacting out of habit or conditioning. Therefore, through mindfulness, we are cultivating a way of being that is open, curious, and non-reactive. We are learning to be present with our experiences, without adding the layer of judgment that can cloud our perceptions and limit our ability to respond effectively.

Obviously, struggles with trauma may require the services of a professional. However, here are some useful steps for times between therapy.

Beginning a Mindfulness Practice

1) Find a quiet space where you won't be disturbed. Sit in a comfortable position with your back straight and your feet planted on the ground. Close your eyes or gaze softly at a fixed point.

2) Begin by taking a few deep breaths. Allow yourself to settle into the present moment and become aware of your body.

3) Focus your attention on your breath. Notice the sensation of the breath as it enters and leaves your body. If your mind starts to wander, gently bring your attention back to your breath.

4) Expand your awareness of your body. Notice any physical sensations, such as tension or discomfort. Allow yourself to feel these sensations without judgment or resistance.

5) Allow any thoughts or emotions that arise to be present without pushing them away or getting caught up in them. Simply observe them with curiosity and compassion.

6) Bring your attention back: If you find yourself getting overwhelmed, bring your attention back to your breath. Use the breath as an anchor to return to the present moment.

7) Practice this for a few minutes each day, gradually increasing the length of your practice over time.

Once the basic bedrock of the garden is made, then it is possible to add the other elements that make a garden possible. The more fruitful the garden, the more these elements are incorporated.

Soil: Compassion

Without compassion, our mindfulness practice can become cold and analytical, lacking in warmth and humanity. Compassion is a fundamental aspect of mindfulness practice, one necessary for our survival as a species. In order to develop true mindfulness, we must cultivate a deep and abiding sense of compassion for ourselves and for all beings.

As the foundation of all ethical behavior, compassion is what allows us to connect with others on a deep level, to feel their suffering as our own, and to respond with wisdom and love.

Compassion is also the key to our own happiness and well-being. When we cultivate compassion for ourselves, we are able to recognize our own limitations and mistakes with greater patience and understanding. We are able to treat ourselves with the same kindness and care that we would offer to a dear friend or loved one. And when we cultivate compassion for others, we are able to create deep and meaningful connections with those around us, based on a shared sense of love and compassion.

In short, compassion is at the heart of mindfulness practice. It is what allows us to connect with others, to feel their suffering as our own, and to respond with wisdom and love. It is the foundation of all ethical behavior, and the key to our own happiness and well-being. Here are some specific ways that practicing compassion can facilitate healing from trauma in the brain:

1) **Regulation of the stress response:** Trauma can result in a hypersensitive stress response, which can make it difficult to cope with everyday stressors. Compassion-based practices can help to regulate the stress response by activating the parasympathetic nervous system, which is responsible for the "rest and

digest" response. This can lead to a decrease in stress hormones like cortisol and an increase in feelings of relaxation and calm.

2) **Activation of reward pathways:** Trauma can lead to a decrease in activity in the brain's reward pathways, which can contribute to symptoms of depression and anhedonia (the inability to experience pleasure). Compassion-based practices can activate these reward pathways, leading to an increase in feelings of pleasure and well-being.

3) **Strengthening of neural connections:** Trauma can result in a decrease in neural connections in the brain, particularly in areas related to emotion regulation and social connection. Compassion-based practices can strengthen these neural connections by increasing activity in these areas of the brain.

4) **Decrease in rumination:** Trauma can lead to persistent negative thoughts and feelings, which can contribute to symptoms of anxiety and depression. Compassion-based practices can help to decrease rumination by promoting acceptance and self-compassion.

The Dalai Lama has outlined several specific steps to practice compassion, which can be helpful for those who are seeking to develop greater compassion in their own lives.

How to Foster Compassion

1) **Cultivate an awareness of suffering:** The first step in cultivating compassion is to become more aware of the suffering of others. This means paying attention to the world around us and recognizing the struggles and challenges that others are facing.

2) **Develop empathy:** The next step is to develop a sense of empathy towards others. This means putting ourselves in their shoes, and imagining what it might be like to experience their suffering firsthand.

3) **Recognize our interconnectedness:** The Dalai Lama emphasizes the importance of recognizing that we are all interconnected, and that the suffering of one person affects us all. By recognizing our interconnectedness, we can develop a greater sense of responsibility and compassion towards others.

4) **Practice kindness:** The Dalai Lama encourages us to practice kindness towards others, even in small ways. This might mean offering a smile or a kind word, or performing a random act of kindness for someone in need.

5) **Practice mindfulness:** Mindfulness is a crucial component of compassion practice, as it allows us to be present with our experiences in a non-judgmental way. By practicing mindfulness, we can cultivate a greater sense of awareness and empathy towards others.

6) **Cultivate a sense of altruism:** Finally, the Dalai Lama encourages us to cultivate a sense of altruism, or a deep and abiding desire to benefit others. This means putting the needs of others before our own, and working to alleviate the suffering of those around us.

After a while, you will get a sense of whether the soil is rich or poor. By following these steps, we can begin to cultivate greater compassion in our own lives, and develop a deeper and more meaningful connection with the world around us. However, if we focus too much on the suffering of other beings, then this makes us unbalanced. Such concern should be complemented by the delight we can take in others.

Sunshine: Delight

Dr. Van der Kolk highlights the importance of finding delight as a component of healing from trauma. Remember, these symptoms of trauma can include hypervigilance, anxiety, depression, dissociation, and a sense of disconnection from oneself and others. We can become stuck in a state of hyperarousal or shutdown.

Finding delight is an important part of healing from trauma because it helps to activate the parasympathetic nervous system, which is responsible for calming the body and reducing feelings of stress and anxiety. When we experience delight, our brains release neurotransmitters such as dopamine, which can help to counteract the negative effects of trauma on the brain and nervous system.

In addition to its physiological benefits, finding delight can also help to promote a sense of safety and security. Engaging in activities that bring us joy and pleasure can help to restore a sense of connection to our mind and promote a sense of safety and well-being in our body.

It's worth noting that finding delight can look different for everyone. For some people, it might mean engaging in physical activity or creative pursuits, while for others, it might mean spending time with loved ones or indulging in a favorite hobby. Whatever form it takes, the key is to engage in activities that bring us joy and pleasure, and to do so in a mindful and intentional way.

Through our compassion for the suffering of other beings, we are also planting a seed to take delight in their well-being, but this also needs to be practiced. A traumatized brain is honed into any signal of possible danger and, leveraging the effects of neuroplasticity, we can find delight and feel anxious when appropriate.

In this part of the chapter, we are going to build a "delight radar". The idea is that, the more we practice, the better our radar. The better our radar, the more it picks up delight.

How to Build a Delight Radar

1) **Pay attention:** Be present and mindful in your daily life, noticing the small moments of joy and delight that might otherwise go unnoticed.

2) **Cultivate curiosity:** Approach the world with a sense of curiosity and wonder, and be open to experiencing delight in unexpected places.

3) **Share your delight:** When you experience something that brings you joy, share it with others. This can amplify the feeling of delight and create a sense of connection and community.

4) **Look for beauty:** Seek out the beauty in the world around you, whether it's in nature, art, or human interaction.

5) **Practice gratitude:** Cultivate a sense of gratitude for the small things that bring you joy and delight, and express that gratitude through writing, meditation, or other practices.

6) **Create rituals:** Establish small rituals or practices that help you tune in to the delights of daily life, whether it's taking a walk in nature, savoring a cup of tea, or journaling about moments of joy.

Water: Koans

Yes, Koans are a form of mindfulness practice. A Koan is a paradoxical statement or question that is used in meditation to help the practitioner reach a state of enlightenment. The purpose of a Koan is to disrupt the mind's normal way of thinking and to encourage a shift in consciousness.

Koans are designed to be unanswerable through rational thought alone, and thus require the practitioner to let go of their logical mind and allow the answer to emerge from a deeper level of awareness. In this way, Koans can be seen as a form of mindfulness practice that cultivates non-judgmental awareness, present-moment attention, and a deep sense of curiosity and inquiry.

To practice with a Koan, the practitioner is asked to focus their attention on the Koan and to contemplate its meaning deeply. The process of contemplation involves sustained attention to the Koan, letting go of any preconceived notions or beliefs, and allowing the mind to become open and receptive to the wisdom that emerges.

One common Koan is "What is the sound of one hand clapping?" This Koan is designed to be unanswerable through rational thought alone, and requires the practitioner to go beyond logical thinking and enter a state of pure awareness.

Another example of a Koan is, "What did your face look like before you were born?" This Koan is intended to help the practitioner recognize the impermanence of their self-identity and to encourage them to connect with their true nature beyond the limitations of the ego.

In Zen Buddhism, Koans are used as a tool for awakening and self-discovery. They are considered a powerful practice for cultivating mindfulness, awareness, and wisdom. Through regular practice with Koans, practitioners can develop a deeper understanding of themselves and the nature of reality.

Getting Started With Koans

1) **Find a teacher:** Koan practice is typically done under the guidance of a teacher who has experience with Koans and can offer guidance and support. Look for a Zen teacher in your local area, or consider joining an online Zen community that offers Koan practice.

2) **Establish a regular meditation practice:** Before beginning with Koans, it's important to have a regular meditation practice. Start by sitting for 10-15 minutes a day and gradually increase the time as you become more comfortable with the practice.

3) **Choose a Koan:** Koans are typically chosen by the teacher and assigned to the student. However, you can also explore Koans on your own and choose one that resonates with you. Look for a Koan that is challenging but not overwhelming.

4) **Sit with the Koan:** Once you have chosen a Koan, sit with it in meditation. Start by focusing your attention on the Koan and contemplating its meaning. As thoughts arise, acknowledge them and return to the Koan.

5) **Engage with the Koan:** Engage with the Koan throughout the day, not just during meditation. Consider the Koan's meaning in relation to your daily life and experiences. Ask yourself how the Koan can be applied to your life.

6) **Meet with your teacher:** Regularly meet with your teacher to discuss your progress with the Koan. The teacher may offer guidance or suggest adjustments to your practice.

7) **Let go of attachment:** Koan practice is not about finding an answer or solving a problem. It's about cultivating a state of mind that is open and receptive to insight and wisdom. Let go of any attachment to finding a solution and trust in the process.

8) **Persist:** Koan practice can be challenging, but it's important to persist. It can take months or even years to fully engage with a Koan and reach a state of insight. Trust in the process and stay committed to the practice.

We might say that the last part is one of the most significant, and most difficult, pieces of advice. All of these practices involve discipline, commitment, concentration, and patience.

Yet, who is not emboldened by a beautiful garden?

Bonus: How to Meditate for Joy

In *The Book of Joy*, which is a dialogue between the Dalai Lama and Desmond Tutu, there is a meditation for the bumpy parts of the road of life. It adopts the title, "The Eight Pillars" and supplements what Dr. Bessel van der Kolk recommends.

1) **Sit in a comfortable position:** place your hands on your lap with crossed or folded legs.

2) **Focus on your breathing:** Take several deep, long breaths through your nose. Let your body relax. Reflect briefly on the pleasure of this, and let your body relax even further, and notice your heart feel lighter.

3) **Let your problem come to mind:** Reflect on what is causing you pain, be it a person, a situation, or a challenge.

4) **Perspective:** Try to step back from your problem and see it from a wider perspective, like you were trying to watch a film of your life, or if you were watching

yourself from the perspective of an astronaut. If the problem does not shrink, try broadening the perspective of time. Will this matter in a year? Will it matter in a decade?

5) **Humility:** If the problem does not shrink from another perspective or a larger time-frame, remember that you are part of a human population that is many billions in number. They, too, suffer and struggle as you. No one is exempt from this condition. Our suffering is a part of the unfolding nature of life, and we rely on each other as interdependent beings, so our suffering is a sign of how profoundly interconnected we all are. This connection makes us better able to respond, to feel the sweetness of appreciation and gratitude for who and what helps us survive. This can give us great strength.

6) **Humor:** With the strength we gain through humility, we can access the power of humor. We can smile about our frailties, laugh at life's foibles, and we can laugh at the absurdity of profoundly difficult situations. Laughter is the saving grace of human drama, as it allows us to accept life as it is, even as we aspire to make it better.

7) **Acceptance:** If we are able to accept that we cannot know all the factors that have led to our struggles, and that we are powerless to change them all, we create a paradox: we accept in order to change. The more reality we can accept, the more we are able to love.

8) **Forgiveness:** Acceptance of our troubles leads to self-forgiveness. Self-forgiveness naturally leads to other-forgiveness. Hopefully, this leads to world-forgiveness.

9) **Gratitude:** Think of three or more people or things that you are grateful for, and see how you can become closer to them. Feel that this gratitude radiates from your heart.

10) **Generosity:** gratitude for what we have naturally extends into a willingness to give to others. If our own cup is full, then the question changes from "How can I fill my cup" to "What gifts can I give to others?" When we give joy to others, we experience true joy ourselves.

Chapter 2

THE BODY

The Story of Sherry

Sherry is one of Dr. Van der Kolk's patients. I've included this story because it is a powerful and poignant example of how someone can become profoundly disconnected from their body.

Sherry arrived to see Dr. Van der Kolk with her arms covered in scabs, and confided in him that picking them gave her relief from feeling numb. Although the physical sensations made her feel more alive, she was deeply ashamed of her addiction to these actions. She had tried to stop, but couldn't. She had consulted with many mental health professionals before Dr. Van der Kolk and had been repeatedly questioned about her "suicidal behavior." She was even involuntarily hospitalized by a psychiatrist, who refused to treat her unless she could promise to never pick at herself again. However, in my experience, and supported by Dr. Bessel van der Kolk, patients who engage in self-harm, like Sherry, are just trying to make themselves feel better in the only way they know.

This is a difficult concept for many people to grasp. The most common response to distress is to seek out people we like and trust to help us and give us the courage to carry on. We learn these ways of regulating our feelings from the first moment someone feeds us when we're hungry, covers us when we're cold, or rocks us when we're hurt or scared. However, Sherry had no one to turn to.

If no one has ever looked at you with loving eyes or broken out in a smile when they see you, and if no one has rushed to help you, then you need to discover other ways of taking care of yourself. You are likely to experiment with anything–such as drugs, alcohol, binge-eating, or cutting–which offers some kind of relief.

Sherry dutifully came to every appointment and answered Dr. Van der Kolk's questions with great sincerity. However, they were not making the sort of vital connection that is necessary for therapy to work. Sherry was still frozen and uptight.

He suggested that she see a massage therapist, whose name is Liz. During their first meeting, Liz positioned Sherry on the massage table and then moved to the end of the table, gently holding Sherry's feet. Sherry lay there with her eyes shut when she suddenly exclaimed in a state of panic, "Where are you?" Despite Liz being right there with her hands on Sherry's feet, Sherry had somehow lost track of her. Dr. Van der Kolk was shocked.

As a professional, his training had primarily focused on understanding and insights, ignoring the significance of the living, breathing body, which represents the core of who we are as individuals. Sherry was aware that picking at her skin was a harmful behavior that was linked to her experiences of neglect. The fact that she understood the root of the urge did not assist her in controlling it, however. Sherry's experience led Dr. Van der Kolk to learn about the severe disconnection from the body that many individuals with histories of trauma and neglect experience as a result of their trauma and neglect.

Trauma and the Body

As we can see from the story of Sherry, trauma can devastate the connection we have with our bodies. Dr. Van der Kolk claims that this partly has to do with how we feel our most devastating emotions: they are often felt as gut-wrenching sensations and heartbreak. These are felt in the body. When emotions are primarily processed in the mind, we retain a degree of comfort and control. However, when we experience the sensation of our chest caving in or being punched in the gut, it becomes unbearable.

In these moments, human beings go to great lengths to get rid of these overwhelming, visceral feelings. This may include desperately clinging to another person, numbing ourselves with drugs or alcohol, or resorting to self-injury to replace the agony of emotions with definable sensations, as in the case with Sherry. How many mental health issues, ranging from drug addiction to self-destructive behavior, arise from attempts to cope with the excruciating physical pain of our emotions? The answer is many.

It is important to get to grips with some of the more regularly found effects that can have a negative impact to assess the seriousness of trauma on the body. Here are some of the effects of trauma on the body, as described by Dr. Van der Kolk:

Some Effects of Trauma on the Body

Dysregulation of the nervous system: Trauma can dysregulate the autonomic nervous system, which controls many of the body's automatic functions, such as heart rate, breathing, and digestion. This can result in a range of physical symptoms, such as rapid heartbeat, shortness of breath, and digestive problems.

Chronic pain: Trauma can increase the risk of chronic pain by sensitizing the nervous system to pain signals. This can result in physical symptoms such as headaches, muscle tension, and joint pain.

Immune system dysfunction: Trauma can compromise the immune system, making individuals more susceptible to infections and other illnesses. This is thought to be due in part to the chronic stress and inflammation that can result from trauma.

Hormonal dysregulation: Trauma can dysregulate the hormonal system, which can lead to a range of physical symptoms and health problems. For example, trauma can disrupt the production of cortisol, a hormone that helps the body to manage stress.

Increased risk of chronic disease: Trauma has been linked to an increased risk of chronic diseases such as heart disease, diabetes, and autoimmune disorders. This is thought to be due in part to the chronic stress and inflammation that can result from trauma.

Evolutionary Theory for Why These Effects Occur

Observations that trauma affects the body has been around since Darwin, though he did not use the term "PTSD" (the diagnostic category was not established until the 20th century).

However, he did write about the physiological and emotional responses to traumatic experiences. In his book *The Expression of the Emotions in Man and Animals*, Darwin suggested that when an animal encounters a threat, its body goes through a series of physiological changes that prepare it for action. These changes include an increase in heart rate and respiration, a release of adrenaline, and a redirection of blood flow to the muscles. If Darwin's theory is correct, then the solution lies in discovering ways to help people modify the sensory landscape of their bodies.

If the animal is able to successfully escape from the threat, these physiological changes gradually subside, and the animal returns to a state of equilibrium.

However, if the animal is unable to escape, or if the threat is ongoing or repeated, the physiological changes may become chronic, leading to symptoms such as anxiety, hypervigilance, and avoidance. Darwin referred to this state as "terror," and he suggested that it could have long-term effects on an animal's physical and mental health.

While Darwin's understanding of PTSD was limited by the scientific knowledge available in his time, his observations of the connection between emotions and physical responses to stress laid the groundwork for later research on trauma and its effects on the body and mind. It was only until very recently that healing practices in the West have taken seriously the body's role in healing trauma, which other parts of the world already have.

Although anger, fear, and anxiety are known to impair reasoning ability, many treatment programs still neglect the importance of first activating the brain's safety system before attempting to encourage new modes of thinking. It is crucial to preserve activities such as chorus, physical exercise, play, and other forms of movement and enjoyable engagement in school, work, and after-work schedules. All of these forms of exercise rely on building interpersonal rhythms, visceral awareness, and communication, which can help shift people out of fight/flight states, and increase their ability to manage relationships.

In this part of the chapter, we are going to delve into different kinds of exercises.

Breathwork

We often take breathing for granted and do it automatically. However, if we consciously control our breath, we can achieve something. By using measured breathing techniques, we can regulate our state of mind and transition from an agitated state to a calm one. In a panic attack, our breathing is completely unregulated, short, and sharp. This means breathwork is a valuable tool for healing from trauma, as it can effectively regulate the nervous system and alleviate feelings of anxiety and overwhelm that frequently occur after a traumatic experience. It is also the simplest.

Pranayama

One example of the kind of breathwork we can do is Pranayama, a type of slow and deep breathing, which originated in Hindu culture and is commonly taught in yoga classes or by licensed breathwork practitioners. The diaphragm, located at the bottom of the lungs, is the most efficient muscle for breathing and performs about 80 percent of the work for people with healthy lungs. Do you breathe from your chest, mostly? Try to breathe from your diaphragm and see what happens. Studies have shown that pranayamic breathing can reduce the frequency of asthma attacks, medication requirements, stress, and anxiety while improving autonomic and higher neural center functioning and physical health, so there is a carrot waiting for you. Why does this happen?

Deep breathing exercises activate the parasympathetic nervous system, which is responsible for rest and relaxation. As a result, breathwork can decrease the levels of stress hormones, including cortisol and adrenaline, in the body, promoting a sense of tranquility and calmness.

It is straightforward to practice pranayamic breathing: you can sit up or lie down with your hands on your belly. Inhale slowly, allowing your belly and ribs to expand, and then exhale and release everything. It's recommended to practice three to five (or up to 10) deep breaths every morning, when stressed, and before bed daily for three weeks to see the benefits. Eventually, your limbic brain will respond to your breath.

Furthermore, breathwork can foster a sense of grounding and connection to the present moment. Trauma frequently causes individuals to feel disconnected from their body and the present, resulting in feelings of dissociation or numbness. However, by focusing on their breath and bodily sensations, individuals can cultivate a sense of presence and connection to the here and now.

Breathwork exercises can take on many different forms, so feel free to explore different techniques and find what works best for you. It is also important to approach breathwork with patience and self-compassion, as it may take some time to feel the benefits of the practice. However, there are some which require licensed practitioners.

Trauma and Tension Release Exercises

Trauma and tension release exercises (TRE) are a type of therapeutic technique that can help individuals release tension and trauma stored in their bodies. TRE is a relatively new approach to trauma therapy and is based on the understanding that trauma can cause chronic tension in the body's muscles.

The exercises involve a series of simple and gentle movements designed to activate the body's natural reflexes for shaking and trembling. These movements can help to release the built-up tension and stored trauma from the body, promoting relaxation and reducing stress.

TRE exercises can be done both individually and in groups, and are typically taught by a certified TRE practitioner. The exercises are easy to learn and can be done at home or in a private setting once an individual has received proper instruction.

Doing TRE Exercises at Home

Here are some general guidelines for doing TRE exercises at home:

Exercise 1: Stimulate the nervous system.

- ❖ Stand with your feet shoulder-width apart.
- ❖ Lean your weight to one side of your body, balancing on the outer edge of the foot on the side you're leaning toward and on the inner side of the foot on the side, you're leaning away from.
- ❖ Take 2-3 slow, deep breaths.
- ❖ Repeat by leaning toward the other side of your body.
- ❖ Repeat on each side 2-3 times.
- ❖ Stretch and shake it out.

Exercise 2: Fatigue calf muscles.

- ❖ Bring your weight onto one foot and bend your opposite knee.
- ❖ Rise up onto your tiptoes, hold for a few seconds, and then slowly lower your heel back to the floor.
- ❖ Repeat until you feel about 70% fatigued.

❖ Repeat with the other foot.

❖ Stretch and shake it out.

Exercise 3: Fatigue quads and glutes.

❖ Assume a simple chair pose. You can use the wall for support or modify it as needed.

❖ Bring your weight to your heels.

❖ Remain in this position until you feel about 70% fatigued.

❖ Stretch and shake it out.

Exercise 4: Stretch your inner thighs.

❖ Stand with your feet comfortably wider than shoulder-width apart.

❖ Fold your body forward, hinging at the hips, and let your head hang down. You can bend your knees here.

❖ While hanging, take three full, deep breaths with your head in the center of your body.

❖ Shift your weight to one side of your body, bringing your head into alignment with your knee. Take three more full, deep breaths.

❖ Repeat on the other side.

❖ Repeat once more in the center and then slowly come back to standing.

❖ Stretch and shake it out.

Exercise 5: Fatigue the upper thighs.

❖ Sit against a wall and make sure you can see your toes.

❖ Dip your hips down low enough to start to feel a burn, and hold that position until you feel about 70% fatigued.

❖ Stretch and shake it out.

Once you have fatigued your lower body and stimulated the right areas, it will be a good time to begin the final part of the exercises.

Lie down on your back with the heels of your feet touching, so your legs should be open. Slowly try and bring them together. You will notice a slight trembling, which is a good sign. Keep your feet together until the trembling becomes more pronounced. Once the trembling starts to become very noticeable, then place your heels down and relax. It will take a while for the trembling to subside, so stop after 20-30 minutes or so.

Yoga

Yoga is arguably the most popular movement-based practice in the West to heal from trauma. However, it is a holistic system of practice that has been used for thousands of years to promote physical, mental, and spiritual well-being in the East.

The word "yoga" comes from the Sanskrit word "yuj" which means to yoke or unite, and refers to the practice of bringing together body, mind, and spirit in order to achieve a state of balance and harmony. It involves various techniques, such as physical postures, breathing exercises, meditation, and ethical principles, that are designed to promote physical health, mental clarity, emotional balance, and spiritual growth.

The physical postures, or *asanas*, are perhaps the most well-known aspect of yoga. They are designed to stretch and strengthen the muscles, improve flexibility, and enhance overall physical health. Some of the most common postures include downward dog, warrior pose, and tree pose. However, meditation, or *dhyana*, is a key aspect of yoga. If we have already built our shrine and practiced meditation, then this part of yoga should be easier to manage.

Breathing exercises, or *pranayama*, are also an important component of yoga. These exercises are designed to regulate the breath and calm the mind. Examples of pranayama include deep belly breathing, alternate nostril breathing, and *ujjayi* breath. I included breathwork in Chapter 1 as an introduction to this aspect of yoga.

In addition to these practices, yoga also includes ethical principles, or *yamas* and *niyamas*, that are intended to guide practitioners towards a more compassionate and mindful way of living. Examples of *yamas* include non-violence, truthfulness, and non-stealing, while examples of *niyamas* include cleanliness, contentment, and self-discipline.

These are important features of yoga, and whatever practice of yoga you intend to do will be fruitful. Dr. Bessel van der Kolk has specifically recommended a type of yoga called trauma-sensitive yoga (TSY).

Practical Steps to Start Trauma-Sensitive Yoga

Trauma-sensitive yoga, henceforth TSY, is a form of yoga that has been adapted specifically for individuals who have experienced trauma. It incorporates many of the principles of traditional yoga, such as breathwork, meditation, and movement, but is modified to be more gentle, slow, and non-triggering. Below are some practical steps involved in trauma-sensitive yoga.

1) **Creating a safe space:** TSY is typically practiced in a small, quiet room with low lighting and soft music. The teacher creates a sense of safety and trust by setting clear boundaries and emphasizing the importance of self-care and self-regulation. If you are used to

meditating by your shrine, then it's a very short step to make the right kind of space for your yoga practice.

2) **Focusing on body sensations:** TSY places a strong emphasis on body awareness and sensation. The teacher encourages students to notice how their body feels in each posture, and to make adjustments based on their own comfort level.

3) **Allowing for choice and control:** TSY gives students a sense of choice and control over their practice. For example, students are encouraged to modify postures or take breaks if needed. This helps to build a sense of agency and empowerment.

4) **Using props:** TSY often incorporates props such as blankets, blocks, and straps, which can be used to support the body in postures. This helps to create a sense of safety and stability.

5) **Incorporating mindfulness and breathwork:** TSY incorporates mindfulness practices such as breathwork and meditation, which can help students stay present and calm. The teacher may guide students through specific breathing exercises, such as deep belly breathing or alternate nostril breathing.

6) **Avoiding triggering language:** TSY teachers are trained to avoid triggering language or physical adjustments that may be triggering for students who have experienced trauma.

Overall, trauma-sensitive yoga is a gentle, non-invasive form of yoga that can be a powerful tool for healing from trauma. By emphasizing body awareness, choice, and control, TSY helps individuals reconnect with their bodies and build a sense of safety and empowerment. In addition to yoga, Dr. Bessel van der Kolk recommends a variety of physical exercises and activities that can be helpful for healing from trauma.

Martial Arts

There are many types of martial arts, like Qigong. Qigong, also spelled as Chi Kung, is an ancient Chinese practice that involves a combination of physical movements, meditation, and breathing techniques. Much like yoga, it is a holistic system of coordinated body posture and movement, breathing, and meditation used for health, spirituality, and martial arts training.

Regularly practicing martial arts can have a range of positive impacts on your experience of life. Through physical activity and practice, you may experience an improvement in your overall fitness level, including increased strength, flexibility, endurance, and balance. In addition to physical benefits, martial arts also require a high level of body awareness and control, which can be helpful in managing stress and anxiety.

As you progress in your practice, you may also experience an increase in self-confidence and a sense of accomplishment. Moreover, the focus and concentration required in martial arts can translate to other areas of your life, such as work or school, leading to improved performance. Additionally, practicing martial arts can be a useful tool for stress management, as techniques such as breathing exercises and mindfulness can be applied to daily life. Finally, joining a martial arts community can provide a sense of social support and camaraderie, offering opportunities to meet new people and form meaningful connections. This will lend a sense of purpose and meaning to your practice.

The word "qigong" translates to "life energy cultivation" or "breath work," which refers to the belief that qi, the vital life force energy, flows through the body and can be harnessed and cultivated through the practice of qigong. Qigong involves slow, gentle movements that are designed to promote the flow of qi throughout the body, as well as breathing techniques and meditation to help improve mental focus and clarity.

There are many different styles and forms of qigong, each with its own unique set of movements and principles. Some styles are focused on physical health and wellness, while others are geared towards spiritual development or martial arts training. Fundamentally, learning martial arts skills and techniques can give individuals a sense of mastery and control over their bodies and surroundings, which can be empowering and healing.

Below are some practical step-by-step ways in which improving martial arts can help heal trauma.

The First Steps of Martial Arts

1) **Find a qualified instructor:** The first step is to find a qualified martial arts instructor who has experience working with individuals who have experienced trauma. Look for an instructor who understands trauma and is patient and compassionate.

2) **Set achievable goals:** Start by setting achievable goals, such as attending a certain number of classes per week or learning a particular technique. Achieving these goals can give a sense of accomplishment and boost confidence.

3) **Focus on presence:** During class, focus on being present in the moment and fully engaging with the techniques and movements. This can help to increase body awareness and reduce feelings of disconnection.

4) **Practice breathing techniques:** Many martial arts involve breathing techniques that can be helpful for

47

managing stress and anxiety. Practice these techniques outside of class as well, especially when feeling overwhelmed.

5) **Build a supportive community:** Martial arts can provide a sense of community and support. Connect with other students and instructors, and attend workshops or seminars to learn from other practitioners.

6) **Be patient and kind to yourself:** Healing from trauma is a process, and progress may not be linear. Be patient and kind to yourself, and don't push yourself too hard. Remember that the goal is to heal and grow, not to achieve perfection or compare yourself to others.

7) **Consider integrating therapy:** Martial arts can be a helpful complement to therapy, but they are not a substitute. Consider integrating therapy into your healing journey, especially if you are dealing with complex trauma or are struggling with symptoms such as depression or anxiety.

Surfing

As Bleakley (2017) describes:

Every surfer craves the experience of surfing with dolphins, or sitting close to basking sharks in blue-green water. I have surfed with dolphins, seals, sharks and sea snakes. I have sensed the sudden suspension of time – sought by all meditative techniques – deep inside the 'tube'; and been clipped by that same wave, then dragged across a razor-sharp live coral reef as the water curtain falls to the sea god's applause. I have nearly drowned at the hands of powerful waves and saved another from drowning. And I have seen suffering men and women reborn and healed through surfing. (p.1)

Surfing is more than just a sport or a pastime, surfing can be a form of mindfulness. It has also helped people develop a deep connection with the natural world. Many surfers believe that surfing can be a form of mindfulness, a way to cultivate a sense of presence and connection with the present moment.

At its core, surfing is a dance with the ocean. It requires a sense of timing, rhythm, and balance. It is impossible to surf without being in sync with the ocean's movements, feeling the power of a wave, and responding in kind. This dance requires complete focus and concentration, as well as a willingness to surrender control. In the midst of a wave, there is no past or future, only the present moment.

As we already know, focusing on the present moment is a key aspect of mindfulness, which involves cultivating a non-judgmental awareness of one's thoughts, feelings, and sensations. By focusing on the present moment, surfers can let go of distractions and become fully immersed in the experience of surfing. When you're riding a wave, it's hard to think about anything else.

Start Surfing for the First Time

1) **Get the necessary gear:** To start surfing, you will need a surfboard and a wetsuit (if you are surfing in cold water). It is important to choose a board that is appropriate for your skill level and body size.

2) **Find a good location:** Look for a beach that is suitable for beginners and has smaller waves. Check local surf reports to find out the best time and conditions for surfing.

3) **Wear sunscreen:** Protect your skin from the sun's harmful rays by wearing waterproof sunscreen. Apply it generously and reapply after being in the water.

4) **Take a lesson:** Consider taking a surf lesson from a qualified instructor. They can teach you proper technique and help you get started safely.

5) **Start small:** Begin with small waves and gradually work your way up to larger ones as your skills improve.

6) **Surf with a partner:** It is always best to surf with a partner, especially when you are starting out. This ensures that someone is there to help you if you get into trouble.

7) **Stay safe:** Always follow proper surf etiquette and be aware of your surroundings. Check the weather and water conditions before heading out, and know your limits.

8) **Respect the ocean:** The ocean is a powerful force, and it is important to respect it. Don't litter on the beach, don't disturb marine life, and be mindful of the impact you are having on the environment.

The last point is one of the most significant, so it is worthwhile elaborating: surfing also requires a deep connection with the natural environment. The ocean is a force greater than ourselves, and surfing requires us to surrender to its power and respect its majesty. In this way, surfing can be a source of humility and gratitude, as well as a way to connect with something greater than ourselves. The ocean is one of the most powerful forces on earth, and engaging with it helps us appreciate the earth's beauty.

The connection with nature that surfing provides can also be a source of healing and renewal. The ocean, surfers will say, has a way of washing away the day-to-day worries we carry with us, and restoring our sense of peace and calm. Waves come and go, rise and fall, and surfing requires us to be attuned to these natural rhythms. By connecting with the natural flow of the ocean, surfers can learn to be patient and trust in the unfolding of life, as we do with non-judgemental awareness in practicing mindfulness meditation. In addition to these deeper philosophical aspects, surfing is a form of play. Like any form of play, surfing can be joyful, fun, and a source of childlike wonder.

If you happen to live in a land-locked area, no worries! There are plenty of other things you can do. The trick is to try and build a connection with your surroundings. It could be the ocean, it could be a mountain, hill, lake, river, forest, or whatever forms part of your landscape.

Bonus: Other Examples of Physical Exercises

1) **Cardiovascular exercise:** Cardiovascular exercise, such as running or cycling, can be particularly helpful for individuals who have experienced trauma. Research has shown that cardiovascular exercise can help to reduce symptoms of depression and anxiety, improve sleep, and increase overall well-being.

2) **Dance:** Dance can be a powerful tool for healing from trauma because it allows individuals to express themselves through movement. Research has shown that dance can help to reduce symptoms of anxiety and depression, improve body image, and increase self-esteem.

3) **Mindful walking:** Mindful walking involves walking slowly and mindfully, paying close attention to each step and the sensations in the body. This can be a helpful practice for individuals who have experienced

trauma because it can help to ground them in the present moment and reduce feelings of dissociation.

4) **Swimming:** Swimming can be a particularly helpful form of exercise for individuals who have experienced trauma because it provides a sense of weightlessness and can be soothing to the nervous system. Additionally, swimming can be a low-impact form of exercise that is gentle on the joints.

By engaging in regular exercise and physical activity, individuals can build a sense of control, empowerment, and resilience that can help them to cope with the effects of trauma.

And there are so many to choose from! I think it's important to include a few examples, so you can pick what you like.

Healthy Eating

Trauma can also affect the way we eat and drink, so it is important to take into account how trauma changes our dieting habits. For instance, According to the National Center for PTSD (2021), trauma can cause a loss of appetite in some people; the Substance Abuse and Mental Health Services Administration (2014) notes that trauma can lead to the development of disordered eating patterns; while Harvard Health Publishing (2020) explains that trauma can cause some people to turn to food as a way to cope with their emotions. Here are the other basic consequences.

- **Loss of appetite:** Trauma can cause a loss of appetite, particularly in the immediate aftermath of the event. This can lead to weight loss and nutritional deficiencies if it persists.

- **Emotional eating:** On the other hand, some people may turn to food as a way to cope with their emotions.

This can lead to overeating or binge-eating, which can also cause weight gain and nutritional imbalances.

- **Avoidance of certain foods or situations:** Trauma can also cause people to avoid certain foods or situations that remind them of the traumatic event. For example, someone who was in a car accident may avoid driving or riding in cars, which can limit their access to food and lead to nutritional deficiencies.

- **Disordered eating:** In some cases, trauma can lead to the development of disordered eating patterns such as anorexia, bulimia, or binge-eating disorder.

It's important to note that everyone responds to trauma differently, and some people may not experience any significant changes to their diet or eating habits. If you or someone you know is struggling with trauma-related eating issues, it's important to seek professional help from a therapist or other mental health provider.

For a traumatized person, eating healthily can be a challenge, but there are several strategies that can help. Here are some ways that a traumatized person could start eating healthily:

- **Seek professional help:** Trauma can have a profound impact on a person's relationship with food and eating habits. Seeking help from a therapist or other mental health provider can help a person address the underlying issues and develop healthy coping strategies.

- **Establish a routine:** Establishing a routine around meal times can help a person develop a regular eating pattern. This can help regulate their appetite and prevent overeating or undereating.

- **Plan meals and snacks:** Planning meals and snacks in advance can help a person make healthier food choices and avoid impulse eating. It can also ensure that they are getting a balanced and nutritious diet.

- **Focus on whole foods:** Eating a diet rich in whole foods such as fruits, vegetables, lean protein, and whole grains can provide the body with the nutrients it needs to function properly. These foods can also help regulate mood and energy levels.

- **Practice mindfulness:** Mindfulness techniques such as deep breathing or meditation can help a person become more aware of their thoughts and emotions around food. This can help them make healthier choices and reduce emotional eating.

- **Get support from loved ones:** Having a support system of friends and family who can offer encouragement and accountability can be helpful in maintaining healthy eating habits.

There is no one specific food or drink that can cure or ameliorate the symptoms of trauma. However, there are certain foods and drinks that may be helpful in promoting overall physical and mental health, which can in turn help manage the symptoms of trauma. Here are some examples:

- **Omega-3 fatty acids**: Omega-3 fatty acids found in fatty fish, nuts, and seeds have been shown to have anti-inflammatory properties that may help reduce symptoms of depression and anxiety.

- **Complex carbohydrates**: Complex carbohydrates found in whole grains, fruits, and vegetables can help regulate blood sugar levels, which can help stabilize mood and energy levels.

- **Probiotics**: Probiotic-rich foods such as yogurt, kefir, and sauerkraut may help improve gut health, which is linked to overall mental health.

- **Herbal teas**: Certain herbal teas such as chamomile, lavender, and valerian root may help promote relaxation and reduce symptoms of anxiety.

- **Dark chocolate**: Dark chocolate contains compounds such as flavonoids and phenylethylamine, which can help improve mood and promote feelings of well-being.

It's important to note that while these foods and drinks may be beneficial, they should not be considered a replacement for professional help and treatment for trauma. A well-rounded, balanced diet that meets individual nutritional needs is key to overall health and well-being.

Chapter 3

THE SENSES

The capacity of art, music, and dance to circumvent the speechlessness that comes with terror may be one reason they are used as trauma treatments in cultures around the world. –Dr. Bessel van der Kolk

Trauma and Our Senses

The story of Sherry is a reminder of how numb we can become to our bodies, but after being traumatized, our senses can be muted as well.

In his laboratory in Adelaide, Australia, Alexander McFarlane investigated how we can recognize objects without visually inspecting them. Different sensory experiences are transmitted to different parts of the brain and then integrated into one perception of an object's shape, weight, temperature, texture, and position. People with PTSD often have difficulty assembling this picture, according to McFarlane. When our senses are muted, we do not feel alive.

Considering this response to trauma raises an important question: In order to live with the natural flow of feelings and feel secure and complete in one's body, how can traumatized individuals learn to integrate their sensory experiences? While mammals are naturally on guard, in order to feel emotionally close to another human being, our defensive system must temporarily shut down. We must turn off our natural vigilance in order to play, mate, and nurture our young. Dr. Bessel van der Kolk reminds us of a story of how this can happen at a basic level.

He recounts how Steve Gross, the previous director of the play program at the Trauma Center. Steve noticed that children would rarely respond to him if she flashed them a grin while he was carrying a vibrantly colored ball, as an invitation to play. Without any takers, he decided to get creative. Later, he "accidentally" dropped the ball near where a child was. When he went to retrieve it, he would gently nudge the ball toward the child, and, rather than ignoring him, the child pushed it back half-heartedly. After a back-and-forth, it wasn't long before they were both smiling. Steve had established a secure space for social engagement with the child, if a small one, and from these simple, rhythmically attuned movements, a connection emerged.

Part of the healing process is to restore trust in our senses, which trauma has fractured, so patients feel encouraged to notice what they are sensing rather than ignore or numb it. As we mentioned in the previous chapter, our gut feelings provide us with indications of safety, sustenance, and threat, even if we cannot always explain why we feel a certain way. Healing from trauma will mean that patients can carry out physical actions that were interrupted by terror.

Our internal sensations constantly send us subtle messages about the needs of our bodies, and gut feelings help us assess what is happening around us. If you have a positive relationship with your inner sensations and can trust them to provide you with accurate information, you will feel in control of your body, emotions, and self.

Similarly, those who have been severely traumatized may benefit more from simply helping to arrange chairs before a meeting or joining others in tapping out a musical rhythm on the chair seats than from sitting in those same chairs and discussing their life's failures. In this chapter, we will go through some of the ways we can connect to our senses, and become more attuned with ourselves, other people, and our environment, in a way that is euthymic rather than arhythmic.

Theatre

Of all the different modes of art, Dr. Van der Kolk is the fondest of theater. This is mostly because, owing to his work with veterans, it is the form of art he has the most exposure to. For example, he has observed and studied three distinct theater-based trauma treatment programs: Urban Improv in Boston, the Trauma Drama program which it inspired in the Boston public schools and residential centers, and the Possibility Project, led by Paul Griffin in New York City.

Although each program differs in its approach, they all share a fundamental basis of addressing the difficult realities of life and utilizing communal action to bring about transformation. Love and hate, aggression and surrender, and loyalty and betrayal, which are also integral to the experience of trauma, are the stuff that makes up theater.

Theater as a mode of healing is not new, but also a "fashion" that has come back. For centuries, human beings have turned to communal rituals for their most intense and terrifying emotions. Among the oldest forms of recorded theater, ancient Greek theater was based on religious rites that involved dancing, singing, and reenacting mythological stories. In the fifth century B.C.E, the theater had become a central element of civic life, with audiences seated in a horseshoe shape around the stage, allowing them to share emotional experiences together. Playwrights were often the biggest celebrities in ancient Greek culture, for instance.

There is a possibility that Greek drama served as a ritualistic means to reintegrate combat veterans into society. There were six fronts of warfare in Athens at the time Aeschylus wrote *The Oresteia* trilogy, and military service was compulsory, so there would have been many citizens who had experiences of warfare. Even the performers were likely citizen-soldiers. Veterans in the United States returning from war were also given the chance to use theater to heal.

The Trauma Center's Trauma Drama program uses mirroring exercises and trust-building exercises to help traumatized adolescents and veterans establish relationships with themselves and others. The program aims to help participants attune viscerally to someone else's experience and access a full range of emotions and physical sensations. The director's job, like that of a therapist, is to slow things down and help the participants establish a relationship with themselves and their bodies. Theater is presented as a unique way to explore alternative ways of engaging with life.

To raise awareness about the struggles of homeless veterans, the Theater of War program, founded by Bryan Doerries, convinced playwright David Mamet to meet with them weekly and develop a script based on their experiences. Mamet then enlisted actors Al Pacino, Donald Sutherland, and Michael J. Fox to participate in an event called "Sketches of War" in Boston, which raised funds to convert a VA clinic into a shelter for homeless veterans. The experience of standing on stage with professional actors and sharing their memories and poetry proved to be a transformative experience for the

59

veterans, more powerful than any therapy could have provided.

The Theater of War performances were followed by a town hall-style discussion where attendees can share their personal experiences related to the themes of the play. There was a reading of Ajax in Cambridge, Massachusetts, where combat veterans, military wives, and recently discharged men and women spoke about their struggles with sleeplessness, drug addiction, and alienation from their families. Dr. Bessel van der Kolk, when he attended these sessions, noted how electric the atmosphere was, and after the discussion, the audience huddled in the foyer, some crying and holding each other while others engaged in deep conversation.

The founder of Theater of War, Bryan Doerries, believes that anyone who has experienced extreme pain, suffering, or death can easily understand Greek drama and the importance of bearing witness to the stories of veterans.

The other project I mentioned, Paul Griffin's Possibility Project in New York City, does not present actors with prepared scripts. Instead, the cast meets for three hours a week over a non-month period. Together, they write a musical and perform it for a total audience of several hundred. Over the history of the Possibility Project, stretching into its twentieth year, a stable staff has come through, building strong traditions and a company of postgraduates. The postgraduates serve as role models for the next class, who, with the help of professional actors, dancers, and musicians, organize scriptwriting, scenic design, choreography, and rehearsals for the incoming class.

When discussing his theater program for foster-care children, Paul Griffin stated, "The stuff of tragedy in theater revolves around coping with betrayal, assault, and destruction. These kids have no trouble understanding what Lear, Othello, Macbeth, or Hamlet are all about." As Tina Packer puts it, "Everything is about using the whole body and having other bodies resonate with your feelings, emotions and thoughts." Through theater, trauma survivors have the opportunity to connect with one another by deeply experiencing their common humanity.

I am not going to give you a basic "to-do" list when starting a theater gig. Hopefully, I have convinced you that it is a worthwhile activity. If I have not, there are a host of other art forms that we can do, which are listed in the sections below.

Painting

Bob Ross, the beloved American painter and TV host, experienced a great deal of trauma during his time in the military. He witnessed the horrors of war firsthand and was stationed in a morgue, where he was responsible for the grim task of cleaning the bodies of fallen soldiers.

After leaving the military, Ross discovered a passion for painting and began to use his art as a way to cope with the trauma he had experienced. He found that the act of painting provided him with a sense of calm and allowed him to escape from the negative thoughts and emotions that were plaguing him. He decided to share his insight with others, and developed a hugely popular show called "The Joy of Painting" on YouTube.

Ross' painting philosophy was simple: you need a few tools, a little instruction, and a vision in your mind. With a blank canvas, you can make magic. By focusing on the process of creating something beautiful, Ross was able to find a sense of purpose and meaning in his life, which helped him to heal from the trauma of his past.

Aside from creating feelings of happiness and calm, one of the reasons Dr. van der Kolk recommends painting, like other forms of art, is expression: it helps to access and communicate emotions and memories that may be difficult to put into words.

Painting, as a form of nonverbal expression, can provide a way to access and release these stored emotions and memories in a way that is beautiful. Painters can access and express emotions and memories, stimulate the prefrontal cortex, and manage stress as part of a holistic approach to healing from trauma.

One famous painter who described how painting helped them to heal is Frida Kahlo. Kahlo was a Mexican painter who is best known for her self-portraits, many of which depict her experiences with physical and emotional pain. Yet, she did not enter into the world of art on a bed of roses, but a terrible accident.

Frida and her boyfriend, Gomez Arias, were riding a bus on September 17, 1925 when it collided with a trolley, leaving Frida with severe injuries. Her spinal column, collar bone, ribs, pelvis, and leg were all broken, and an iron handrail punctured her abdomen and uterus. In the aftermath of the accident, Frida felt as though everything she had known had fallen apart. However, during the many months it took for her body to heal, she underwent a profound transformation in her views on life and art. Although she was confined to bed and saw very few visitors, Frida began to paint more and more. Her loneliness became the catalyst for a new form of expression: she told her story, and shared her experience, through painting.

Kahlo's paintings were a way for her to process and express her emotions and experiences, particularly those related to her chronic physical pain and disability. She painted herself because she was often alone, and the subject matter she was most intimate with. In a sense, painting for Kahlo was a kind of therapy: it allowed her to confront her deepest feelings of pain, and beautify them.

Kahlo's work has since become iconic for its raw emotional power and its ability to capture the complexities of the human experience. Her paintings continue to inspire and resonate with people around the world. Not all of us can, or even should, aspire to her success, but we can all learn how to express ourselves through painting.

A Beginner's Guide to Painting

1) **Choose your medium:** There are several painting mediums to choose from, such as watercolors, acrylics, oils, or gouache. Each medium has its own unique characteristics and requires different techniques and materials. Research the different mediums and decide which one you want to start with.

2) **Get your supplies:** Once you have chosen your medium, you will need to get the necessary supplies. Basic supplies typically include paint, brushes, canvas or paper, a palette, and paint thinner (if using oil paints). There are also many optional supplies you can purchase, such as mediums, varnishes, or specialized brushes, but you can start with the basics.

3) **Learn the basics:** Start with the basics of color theory, composition, and brush techniques. Watch online tutorials, read books, or attend classes to learn the fundamentals of painting.

4) **Start painting:** Once you have the supplies and some basic knowledge, start painting! Start with simple

projects to build your skills and confidence. Don't be afraid to experiment and try new techniques.

5) **Develop a routine:** Consider setting up a dedicated workspace for painting and develop a regular painting routine that works for you. This can help you stay organized, focused, and motivated to continue practicing.

6) **Experiment with different techniques:** Try experimenting with different techniques, such as layering, blending, or texture, to find your own unique style. Don't be afraid to make mistakes or try new things.

7) **Learn from other artists:** Look to other artists for inspiration and learning opportunities. Attend art exhibitions, visit museums, and study the work of other painters to gain insights into different styles and techniques.

8) **Join a painting community:** Joining a painting community can provide you with valuable feedback, support, and opportunities to learn from other painters. Consider joining a local art club or online painting group.

9) **Practice regularly:** Painting, like any skill, takes practice to master. Dedicate time each week to painting, and try to challenge yourself with more complex projects over time.

10) **Get feedback:** It can be helpful to get feedback from other artists or art enthusiasts. Share your work with friends, family, or online communities to get feedback and support.

11) **Take breaks:** Painting can be mentally and physically tiring. Take breaks when needed to rest your eyes, stretch your body, and clear your mind. This can help you avoid burnout and maintain your passion for painting.

12) **Have fun:** Most importantly, have fun! Painting should be an enjoyable and fulfilling experience, so don't get too caught up in trying to create the perfect masterpiece. Embrace the process and enjoy the journey.

13) **Watch Bob Ross:** If you are finding any of the steps particularly difficult, then Bob Ross will be a very helpful teacher.

Dancing

Dancing is perhaps the most ancient form of art in human society, and culture is all the worse when it has no form of dance. It is not merely through movement that a person can tap into the physical sensations and emotions associated with trauma and begin to process and integrate those experiences in a more embodied way, it has to be given a rhythm and a community. Dancing, though it is primarily a form of movement, helps us to connect. However, if you need some encouragement, here are the benefits of dancing that you can look forward to.

The Benefits of Dancing

Expressive movement: Dancing can be a form of expressive movement that allows individuals to express emotions and release tension. Trauma can be stored in the body as physical tension, and dancing can help to release that tension and promote relaxation.

- **Regulation of the nervous system**: Trauma can dysregulate the nervous system, leading to symptoms such as anxiety, hypervigilance, and dissociation. Dancing can help to regulate the nervous system by providing a structured, rhythmic activity that can promote a sense of safety and calm.

- **Positive social interaction**: Dancing can be a social activity that promotes positive social interaction and connection with others. This can be particularly helpful for individuals who have experienced trauma, as social support is an important factor in healing from trauma.

- **Mindfulness and embodiment**: Dancing can be a mindfulness practice that promotes embodiment, or a sense of being present and connected to one's body. Trauma can cause individuals to dissociate from their bodies, and dancing can help to promote a sense of connection and embodiment.

- **Joy and pleasure**: Dancing can be a joyful and pleasurable activity that promotes positive emotions and feelings of well-being. Trauma can be associated with feelings of fear, sadness, and despair, and dancing can help to promote positive emotions and a sense of enjoyment.

- **Connection**: By participating in a group dance or movement class, individuals can feel a sense of belonging and connection not only with themselves, but also with others, which can help to counteract the feelings of isolation and disconnection that often accompany trauma.

Van der Kolk is not the only one to write about the importance of dancing. The famous mystic, Rumi, wrote extensively about the spiritual and transformative power of dance, and his poetry often includes references to whirling dervishes and other forms of ecstatic dance.

Another author who has explored the philosophical and cultural significance of dance is the French philosopher, Maurice Merleau-Ponty. In his book, *Phenomenology of Perception*, he argues that dance is a fundamental mode of human expression, and that it reveals important aspects of our embodied experience in the world.

Other writers who have explored the theme of dance include the American poet Walt Whitman, the British novelist Virginia Woolf, and the German philosopher Friedrich Nietzsche. Each of these writers approached the topic of dance from a unique perspective, offering insights into its aesthetic, cultural, and philosophical dimensions. So, what else are you waiting for?

Let's Dance!

Learning to dance can be a fun and rewarding experience! Here are some steps you can take to get started:

1) **Decide what kind of dance you want to learn:** There are many types of dance styles to choose from, such as ballet, salsa, hip hop, ballroom, tap, and more. Think about what kind of music and movements you enjoy, and what your goals are for learning to dance.

2) **Find a dance studio or class:** Once you've chosen a dance style, look for local dance studios or classes that offer instruction in that style. You can search online or in your community for classes.

3) **Dress appropriately:** Wear comfortable clothing that allows you to move freely and supportive shoes that are appropriate for the style of dance you are learning. This can help you avoid discomfort and improve your performance.

4) **Attend a beginner's class:** Most dance classes will offer a beginner's class that will teach you the basics of the style you have chosen. This is a great way to get started and learn the fundamentals of dance.

5) **Warm-up and stretch:** Before you begin dancing, it's important to warm up your muscles and stretch to prevent injury. This can include basic stretches, such as hamstring stretches or shoulder rolls, or a short cardio workout to get your blood flowing.

6) **Practice at home:** Practice makes perfect! Try to practice what you've learned in class at home. You can also watch videos online to learn more about the dance style and how to improve your technique.

7) **Listen to your body:** Pay attention to your body and don't push yourself beyond your limits. Take breaks when needed, and don't force yourself to perform movements that cause pain or discomfort.

8) **Focus on technique:** As you learn new dance moves, focus on proper technique to ensure you are performing the movements correctly. This can help you avoid injury and improve your overall performance.

9) **Record yourself:** Recording yourself while you practice can be a helpful way to review your technique and identify areas for improvement. You can also use these recordings to track your progress over time.

10) **Attend performances:** Watching live dance performances can be inspiring and can provide you with new ideas and techniques to incorporate into your own dancing.

11) **Dance with a loved one:** Dancing is a special technique of moving to foster connection. Try it out

with a loved one, and you're bound to find joyful results.

Remember, the most important thing is to have fun and enjoy the process of learning to dance. With dedication and practice, you can become a great dancer!

Writing

Each of us is living a story that we have inherited, and each of us has a story to tell. We have had stories handed down, and we will hand down other stories. It is possible to find out more about the story we are living through, and living with, by writing. If we become better writers, it is possible to share our story, foster empathy, and not only help us make sense of our own experiences and emotions, but also those of others. Writing, as a form of self-expression, can provide a way to access and release these stored emotions and memories that are initially opaque.

Although Dr. Van der Kolk has said that verbal expression may be complicated, and that we should investigate non-verbal ways to overcome trauma, writing allows us to take our time and engage with a broader community. Additionally, writing can help individuals develop a coherent narrative of their experiences, which can be empowering and help reduce feelings of helplessness and disorientation that are common with trauma.

Part of the reason why writing helps with these things is that it can help activate the prefrontal cortex, the part of the brain responsible for decision-making, problem-solving, and emotional regulation. Trauma can affect the prefrontal cortex, making it harder to regulate emotions and make decisions.

Reading

If there is a single adage that writers all follow, it is that they read. How good one can be as a writer depends on how well one can read. It can take years to write well, and, if one is not so ambitious, then we can all begin to become a better reader by immersing ourselves in the world of another. By exploring the specific world of someone else, a story has the power to touch our own. It foregrounds the utter complexity of the human experience that can leave us baffled, while also offering a deeper understanding of the nuances of human emotion and behavior.

When we read, we also absorb the writing style and techniques of other writers, and this not only helps us to write, but it also helps to communicate. This will feature strongly in the last chapter. For now, I want to focus on the practical reason for reading that is involved in the healing of trauma: catharsis.

Catharsis is a term that originates from Aristotle's Poetics, where he described it as the emotional release or purification that occurs in the audience through experiencing a tragic play. According to Aristotle, the audience feels a sense of emotional relief and purification by watching the tragedy, which leads to catharsis.

Stephen King, a popular contemporary author, also believes that reading can induce catharsis. In his book *On Writing: A Memoir of the Craft*, King explains that reading allows us to experience emotions in a safe and controlled environment. He believes that reading a well-crafted story can evoke strong emotional reactions in the reader, and this emotional release can be cathartic. If you've ever read King's stories, then you'll know how scary they can be. However, because you are reading, and not in a genuinely threatening situation, it is possible to release the fear that you carry in your body.

Both Aristotle and King suggest that catharsis is achieved through the experience of emotion in a safe environment. In the case of tragic plays, the audience is able to experience intense emotions and empathize with the characters without experiencing the consequences of their actions. Similarly, in reading, the reader is able to experience strong emotions and empathize with the characters without experiencing the consequences of their actions in real life.

Reading, therefore, provides a way for us to experience and process our emotions in a safe environment, leading to a sense of emotional release and catharsis. Through reading, we are able to explore our own emotions and experiences in a way that can be healing and transformative. Here's a reading list curated by George Saunders to get you going:

A Short Reading List Compiled by George Saunders

- *In Our Time* by Ernest Hemingway
- *The Complete Works* of Isaac Babel
- *Dispatches* by Michael Herr
- *The Bluest Eye* by Toni Morrison
- *Visions of Gerard* by Jack Kerouac
- *The Collected Tales* of Nikolai Gogol

The Greatest Books of the 20th Century

- *Lolita* by Vladimir Nabokov
- *The Great Gatsby* by F. Scott Fitzgerald
- *In Search of Lost Time* by Marcel Proust
- *Ulysses* by James Joyce
- *Dubliners* by James Joyce

- *One Hundred Years of Solitude* by Gabriel Garcia Marquez
- *The Sound and the Fury* by William Faulkner
- *To The Lighthouse* by Virginia Woolf
- *The Complete Stories* by Flannery O'Connor
- *Pale Fire* by Vladimir Nabokov

If you are an ambitious person who would also like to write, well, then there are two different styles we are going to explore below.

Memoir

Writing facilitators say that it has become abundantly clear how writing can change people: it involves giving attention to the details of your life and experimenting with them by putting them on a page. Therefore, it is not only about learning how to write. It is a tool of awareness, of understanding how the mind works. In order to initiate, pursue, and complete a complex piece of writing, it can make a person better. As we know, past trauma makes for shaky ground, in part, because people struggle with feelings of poor self-esteem, and who find it difficult to express themselves.

For instance, one of the voices against writing a memoir is "self-indulgence". This is a criticism that shuts down people before they even begin. We all have a need to be seen, to be acknowledged, and it is an act of bravery to tell one's story. They are often laboring under devastating internal judgment, and, once alleviated, a person can live more creatively, less anxious and self-destructive, which means greater tolerance and compassion for oneself and others.

Writing an autobiography in a short story style can be a challenging but rewarding experience. Here are some practical steps you can take to get started:

1) **Identify the key moments and themes of your life:** Before you start writing, take some time to reflect on your life and identify the key moments and themes that have shaped you as a person. This could include significant events, relationships, or experiences.

2) **Create an outline:** Once you have identified the key moments and themes, create an outline of your autobiography. This will help you structure your story and ensure that you include all the important details.

3) **Determine your narrative voice:** Decide on the narrative voice that you want to use for your autobiography. Do you want to write in the first person or third person? Will you use a consistent narrative voice throughout the story?

4) **Use vivid and descriptive language:** To bring your story to life, use vivid and descriptive language to help the reader visualize the scenes and emotions you are describing.

5) **Focus on character development:** Since you are writing in a short story style, it's important to focus on character development. Show the reader how you have grown and changed over time.

By following these practical steps and avoiding common pitfalls, you can write an autobiography in a short story style that is engaging, authentic, and inspiring.

Poetry

Mary Oliver, the late American poet, believed that poetry was important because it helps us to pay attention to the world

73

around us. In her essay "Of Power and Time," she wrote that poems feed the hungry, warm the cold, and give a hand to those who are lost.

Oliver suggests that poetry has a transformative power that goes beyond mere words. It has the ability to console, guide, and nourish. Oliver believed that poetry was essential for our spiritual and emotional well-being, and that it helped us to connect more deeply with the world around us.

Furthermore, Oliver believed that poetry was a way of cultivating attention and awareness. She wrote, "Attention is the beginning of devotion." In other words, by paying close attention to the natural world and the small moments of beauty in our everyday lives, we can develop a deeper appreciation for the world around us. Poetry, with its emphasis on language and imagery, can help us to see the world in new and profound ways, and to find meaning and purpose in even the most ordinary experiences.

Writing poetry can be a rewarding and creative form of self-expression. Here are some practical steps you can take to get started:

Writing a Poem

1) **Read poetry:** Start by reading different types of poetry from a variety of poets. This will give you a sense of the different styles, themes, and techniques that are used in poetry.

2) **Practice writing:** Start by writing every day, even if it's just for a few minutes. Set aside time to write and experiment with different styles and techniques.

3) **Elevate the mundane:** Poetry is about beautifying ordinary details of life that we would otherwise ignore. It makes life much more interesting, and far less dull.

4) **Experiment with form and structure:** Poetry can take many different forms and structures. Experiment with different forms such as sonnets, haikus, free verse, and others to see what works best for you.

5) **Use sensory language:** Poetry is all about creating images and emotions with language. Use sensory language to help your readers see, hear, smell, taste, and feel what you're describing.

6) **Revise and edit:** Once you have a draft of your poem, revise and edit it. Read it out loud to see how it flows and if there are any changes you can make to improve it.

7) **Explore different themes:** Poetry can be inspired by a wide range of themes such as love, nature, loss, politics, and more. Experiment with different themes to find what resonates with you and your style.

8) **Find inspiration in your surroundings:** Look around you and draw inspiration from your surroundings. It can be anything from the colors of the sunset to the sound of the wind.

9) **Play with language:** Poetry is all about the use of language. Play with words, metaphors, and similes to create vivid and powerful images that will captivate your readers.

10) **Embrace vulnerability:** Poetry can be an emotional outlet. Don't be afraid to write about your personal experiences, thoughts, and feelings. This vulnerability can make your poetry more relatable and powerful.

11) **Attend poetry events:** Attend poetry readings, workshops, and open mic nights to meet other poets,

learn from their experiences, and get feedback on your own work.

12) **Practice empathy:** Poetry can help us connect with other people and understand their experiences. Practice empathy by putting yourself in someone else's shoes and writing from their perspective.

13) **Read your poetry aloud:** Reading your poetry aloud can help you identify areas where the flow is off or where the language feels clunky. It can also help you practice your delivery if you plan on performing your poetry.

By following these practical steps and avoiding common pitfalls, you can start writing poetry that is unique, expressive, and powerful.

Chorus

Bessel van der Kolk suggests that joining a choir can help with healing from trauma because it involves several components that activate the social-engagement system of the brain, which is essential for healing from trauma. Singing with others creates a sense of connection, belonging, and safety, which can help to counteract the isolation and disconnection that are common in trauma. Additionally, singing involves deep breathing, which can help to regulate the autonomic nervous system and reduce symptoms of anxiety and hypervigilance. Finally, singing in a choir involves synchronized movement and rhythm, which can help to regulate the body and promote a sense of calm and relaxation. Overall, joining a choir can be a powerful tool for healing from trauma, as it provides a safe and supportive environment for individuals to engage in activities that promote connection, regulation, and joy.

Join a Choir

1) **Research choirs in your area:** Look up choirs in your local community or online. You can check local community centers, schools, places of worship, and online directories to find choirs that are open to new members.

2) **Attend a rehearsal:** Once you've found a choir that interests you, find out when their next rehearsal is and attend as an observer. This will give you a sense of the choir's style, repertoire, and level of difficulty.

3) **Contact the choir director:** After attending a rehearsal, reach out to the choir director to express your interest in joining. You can usually find their contact information on the choir's website or social media pages.

4) **Audition:** Some choirs require an audition to join, especially if they have a more advanced level or if they are selective. The choir director will let you know if an audition is necessary and what the requirements are.

5) **Practice and participate:** Once you're accepted into the choir, attend all rehearsals and practice at home to prepare for performances. Get to know the other members and participate in choir events and activities.

6) **Enjoy the experience:** Joining a choir can be a fun and rewarding experience, so enjoy the opportunity to learn new skills, make new friends, and express yourself through music.

7) **Get familiar with music notation:** If you're not familiar with music notation, take some time to learn the basics. This will help you follow along with sheet music during rehearsals and performances.

8) **Stay committed:** Joining a choir requires a certain level of commitment. Make sure you're able to attend all rehearsals and performances, and communicate with the choir director if you have any conflicts.

9) **Take voice lessons:** If you're new to singing or want to improve your vocal technique, consider taking voice lessons. This will help you develop good singing habits and improve your overall sound.

10) **Volunteer:** Many choirs rely on volunteers to help with tasks such as fundraising, marketing, and event planning. Consider volunteering your time and skills to support your choir.

11) **Attend workshops and retreats:** Many choirs offer workshops and retreats to help members improve their skills and bond as a group. Attend these events to deepen your musical knowledge and build relationships with other choir members.

12) **Have fun:** Singing in a choir can be a joyful and uplifting experience, so don't forget to have fun and enjoy the music!

Music

Scientists who study trauma and music have suggested that playing music, and music therapy, can be helpful for individuals dealing with trauma for several reasons.

The brain mechanisms behind music are interesting to note. Playing music activates areas of the brain that have to do with emotional regulation, memory processing, and attention. This is one reason why music helps us connect to our senses and heal from trauma: it activates areas of the brain that have to do with perception, emotion, and memory.

Firstly, music has the ability to activate different regions of the brain that are associated with emotional regulation, memory processing, and attention. One of the reasons why music is so effective at connecting us with our senses is because it activates different parts of the brain that are associated with perception, emotion, and memory. For example, when we listen to music, the auditory cortex of our brain is activated, allowing us to process different elements of the music such as melody, rhythm, and harmony.

In addition to its effects on the brain, music also has the ability to evoke strong emotional responses in listeners. This is because music can be used to express and convey complex emotions in a way that is accessible and relatable to a wide range of listeners. For example, the music of artists such as Bob Dylan, Joni Mitchell, and Leonard Cohen has been praised for its ability to express deep emotional truths and connect with listeners on a visceral level. Therefore, secondly, music therapy can provide a non-verbal means of communication that can help individuals express and process difficult emotions that may be difficult to articulate in words. This can be especially helpful for individuals who have experienced trauma, as they may have difficulty verbalizing their experiences or may feel overwhelmed by their emotions.

Thirdly, music can be a powerful tool for relaxation and stress reduction. This is particularly important for individuals who have experienced trauma, as they may be more likely to experience symptoms of anxiety, depression, and post-traumatic stress disorder (PTSD). Music therapy can help to reduce these symptoms by promoting feelings of calm, relaxation, and well-being.

Finally, music therapy can also provide a sense of connection and community for individuals who have experienced trauma. This can be especially important for individuals who feel isolated or disconnected from others as a result of their experiences.

Overall, music therapy can be a helpful tool for individuals dealing with trauma, as it can provide a safe and supportive environment for emotional processing, non-verbal communication, relaxation, and community building.

Let's Start Playing Music!

Here is a basic list for anyone looking to start playing music at home:

1. **Choose an instrument:** Decide which instrument you want to learn and purchase or rent one. Some popular beginner instruments include guitar, piano, ukulele, and drums.

2. **Get the necessary accessories:** Purchase any necessary accessories for your instrument, such as a tuner, picks, strings, drumsticks, or a music stand.

3. **Find instructional resources:** Look for instructional books, online tutorials, or video lessons to get started. There are many free resources available online for beginners.

4. **Practice regularly:** Set aside time each day or week to practice your instrument. Consistency is key when learning a new skill.

5. **Start with basic chords or scales:** Focus on learning basic chords or scales to build a foundation for more advanced playing. This will help you to develop muscle memory and strengthen your fingers.

6. **Experiment with playing along to music:** Try playing along to your favorite songs or backing tracks

to practice playing with others and to develop your sense of rhythm and timing.

7. **Join a community:** Look for local music groups, online forums, or social media groups to connect with other musicians and get support and feedback on your playing.

8. **Set up a comfortable and inspiring practice space:** Choose a space in your home that is comfortable and conducive to practice, such as a spare room, corner of a living room, or outside area. Make sure the lighting is adequate and the temperature is comfortable for playing.

9. **Warm up before playing:** Just like with any physical activity, it's important to warm up your body before playing an instrument. Stretch your fingers, wrists, and arms before starting to play to prevent injury and improve your playing.

10. **Record and listen to yourself playing:** Recording yourself playing can help you identify areas where you need to improve and track your progress over time. Listening back to your recordings can also be a helpful way to get feedback on your playing and identify areas where you can improve.

11. **Set goals for yourself:** Setting specific goals for what you want to achieve with your playing can help keep you motivated and focused. Whether it's mastering a specific song or technique, or improving your overall playing ability, having clear goals can help you stay on track.

12. **Take breaks and listen to music:** Playing music can be mentally and physically demanding, so it's important to take breaks and give your mind and body

time to rest. Listening to music can also be a great way to inspire and motivate you to keep playing.

13. **Experiment with different styles and genres:** Don't be afraid to try playing different styles and genres of music to find what you enjoy most. Whether it's rock, jazz, classical, or folk, exploring different types of music can help you discover new techniques and expand your musical knowledge.

My hope from this chapter is to suggest how important art is as an integral part of every culture, much like language. Even primitive societies, without any formal religion or mythology, still had some form of artistic expression; whether it be in the form of dance, song, or design (even if only on tools or the human body). This universal nature of art stands in stark contrast to the common belief that art is a luxury item of civilization. Art is, in fact, a driving force in social and individual human development. The loss of art's obvious value is a clear indication of a decline in culture. The emergence of a new form of art or a unique artistic style always signifies a fresh and vibrant mindset, whether it is the work of an individual or a collective effort.

Chapter 4

CONNECTING WITH OTHERS

At the Trauma Center, we offer programs to coach parents in connection and attunement. In addition to these programs, my patients have shared with me many other ways to get in sync, such as choral singing, ballroom dancing, joining basketball teams, jazz bands, and chamber music groups. Engaging in these activities fosters a sense of attunement and communal pleasure. –Dr. Bessel van der Kolk

All the previous chapter's exercises in honing our attention, developing an awareness of self, our habitual thought patterns, cultivating a visceral and self-awareness, practicing being in sync with others, opening the possibility to change the way we communicate. We are better able to focus on areas that have the potential to produce what we are seeking. What is desired in life is compassion, a mutual exchange of giving between oneself and others, and this can happen through communication that is heartfelt.

This final chapter has to do with how we keep in touch with the compassionate part of ourselves in relationships with others. This is the final chapter because, if we have an established practice from the previous chapters, it is much easier to accomplish this. It is in our nature to enjoy giving and receiving compassion, and, so, we can ask two questions: what disconnects us from our compassionate nature? As we have discussed in the previous chapters, when we become disconnected from our mind, body, and senses, then it becomes very difficult to regulate ourselves, and, as a consequence, difficult to become a wholesome part of a community. What empowers us, for example, to stay connected to our compassionate nature so that we can open our hearts, even under the worst circumstances?

The Effect of Trauma on Relationships With Others

Early Attachments

It is difficult to overstate how important our early attachments are for the rest of our lives. These relationships shape not only our expectations of others, but also how much comfort we can experience in the presence of others. Put another way, we are given a relational "map" in our emotional brain, formed by expectations of where we are headed in a given situation, and cannot be reversed by understanding how they were made. Even if we realize, say, that our fear of intimacy is linked to our mother's depression, or her experiences of abuse, this is unlikely to make us open to being happy and trusting with others.

If our early experiences of attachment are fraught or hostile, it may be harder to develop a relational map that allows us to open our hearts to other people. If that is the case, we need to apply efforts to consciously work through it. However, when we overcome negative patterns and cultivate positive ones, there is another side of fear in our intimate relations: many poets write about them beautifully. It shows us that the effort is worthwhile.

Following the examination of the idling brain and the "Mohawk" sense of self (or lack thereof), scientists have turned their focus to another question: what occurs in people with trauma when they engage in face-to-face contact?

After examining the idling brain, Ruth Lanius, a colleague of Van der Kolk's, and her team delved into this question. Interestingly, patients frequently struggled to maintain eye contact, and their distress is evident in their inability to meet the gaze of others. Lanius found that their intense feelings of shame were reflected in abnormal brain activity.

Individuals without trauma and those with trauma showed a marked difference in brain activation when facing direct eye contact. While the prefrontal cortex (PFC) was activated in individuals without trauma, those with trauma displayed no activation in any part of their frontal lobe. Instead, they exhibited intense activation in primitive regions of the emotional brain, which generates self-protective behaviors like startling, hypervigilance, and cowering. They simply shifted into survival mode when faced with direct eye contact, meaning that they perceive someone as a threat rather than as someone who is safe. Trauma can make these distinctions difficult to discern, leading to confusion and uncertainty.

This means we need to go back to the basics of communication for those with trauma: words can be our walls or can be our windows.

How Trauma Affects the Way We Speak

Imagine that there's a rumor that a construction worker is stealing from his workplace. The security guards constantly check his clothes, his lunchbox, and his wheelbarrow, but they can't seem to find anything. They get more and more furious, and invent more and more complicated ways of checking for anything he may have stolen. From a casual glance to a mandatory pocket check, and, finally, a highly advanced and very expensive metal detector just for that employee. Eventually, an entire month goes by and after much wasted time and energy, they give up. They never realized that the employee was stealing the wheelbarrows.

The point of that story is how we sometimes miss the thing that is most obvious. When people are traumatized, they cannot express their feelings very well. If we already communicate in a way that alienates us from ourselves and other people, it is harder for people who have been traumatized because their hearts are closed off. I will call this Heartless Communication.

Speaking With and Without the Heart

Going back to an earlier question, "How do we stay in touch with our compassionate nature, so that we can still open our hearts under difficult circumstances?" I am thinking of people like Etty Hillesum, who remained compassionate even while subjected to the grotesque conditions of a German concentration camp. As Hillesum (1983) wrote in her journal:

> I am not easily frightened. Not because I am brave but because I know that I am dealing with human beings, and that I must try as hard as I can to understand everything that anyone ever does. And that was the real import of this morning: not that a disgruntled young Gestapo officer yelled at me, but that I felt no indignation, rather a real compassion, and would have liked to ask, 'Did you have a very unhappy childhood, has your girlfriend let you down?' Yes, he looked harassed and driven, sullen and weak. I should have

liked to start treating him there and then, for I know that pitiful young men like that are dangerous as soon as they are let loose on mankind. (n.p.)

There is a natural way we can speak and listen that leads us to give from our heart, which helps us connect to ourselves and with another in a way for compassion to flourish. There is a specific approach to communicating—both speaking and listening—that leads us to give from the heart, connecting us with ourselves and with each other, in a way that allows our natural compassion to flourish.

We can call this Heartfelt Communication, a state of compassion where the violent part of ourselves, the part that wants to hurt someone, has subsided. While we may not consider the way we talk to be hurtful, words often lead to hurt and pain, whether for others or ourselves. Words are powerful.

Heartfelt communication requires mindfulness and compassion, something we have begun cultivating in Chapter 1. It helps us to stop repeating habitual or automatic responses, and so our words become conscious and aware responses based on what we are perceiving, feeling, and wanting. It means we are able to express ourselves with honesty and clarity, giving others respectful and empathic attention, thereby avoiding judgment and manipulation. Once we have replaced old patterns of defending, withdrawing, and attacking in the face of judgment or criticism, we can come to see ourselves and other people, our intentions and relationships, in a new light. When we can catch our resistance, defensiveness, and fearfulness, heartless reactions are minimized (and the word "heartless" is a synonym for violence or cruelty), we can access an even deeper level of compassion.

This is not only a matter of how we attend to our own words, but also the words of others: when we listen deeply, not just to what words are used but the sound of someone's voice, then heartfelt communication can foster respect, attentiveness, and empathy which, as noted already, gives us the right conditions to open our hearts. We begin to actually hear the needs of others, to begin to trust. We are more likely to receive what we are truly seeking.

How Do We Begin?

Simply observe the situation at hand, and take note of what others are doing or saying that makes you feel less like expressing yourself, or drains a sense of life's quality. Simply observe, there is no need to judge or evaluate. The key is to note what we like or dislike, and then express what we feel, whether it is hurt, joy, or irritation. Lastly, we identify the value that is connected to emotion. Has it been seen or ignored? When we use heartfelt communication, we need to be aware of these three components: noticing, emotion, and values.

Noticing: There is a difference between observing and evaluating. This means paying attention to the specific behaviors, actions, or situations that are causing our feelings rather than judging or blaming ourselves or others.

Emotions: Once we have made clear observations, we need to identify and express our own feelings. Heartfelt communication encourages people to use clear and simple language to describe their emotions in a non-judgmental way.

Values: Understanding and communicating our own needs and the needs of others is a central concept in heartfelt communication. We are encouraged to identify our own needs and to listen empathetically to the needs of others, without making judgments or assumptions.

Heartfelt Communication in Action

Noticing

The first step of speaking with our heart is to separate noticing from evaluating. We need to notice what we are sensing that is affecting us, without judging what it means. Otherwise, it is difficult to express ourselves clearly and honestly, which allows for change rather than stasis. I'll give an example.

When I was called in to try to understand some communication problems at a school, I noticed that the staff did not say how they felt about their principal's story-telling habit.

In a meeting, I asked the staff what the principal was doing that conflicted with their needs, and one teacher responded with an evaluation, saying that the principal had a "big mouth." Other teachers followed with similar evaluations, making it difficult to pinpoint the specific behaviors that bothered them. When I went to one of the meetings with the principal, I noticed he would tell a story about his time in Vietnam as a war veteran. No one said anything, and so the meetings ran 20 minutes overtime. However, throughout, people looked at their phones, dozed off, or fidgeted. It was not Heartfelt Communication, it was nonverbal condemnation.

We eventually created a list of the principal's behaviors that bothered the staff, such as his tendency to tell stories during meetings about his experiences of war. During a subsequent meeting with the principal and staff, the principal interjected with a story about his storytelling habit. We worked on ways for the staff to let him know when his stories weren't appreciated. It was a challenging process to separate observation from evaluation, but we eventually succeeded in clarifying the specific actions that led to the staff's concerns.

89

Evaluations	Observations
1. The principal has a big mouth.	1. The principal spoke past the time when the meeting was scheduled to end.
2. The principal is inconsiderate.	2. The principal did not notice that people looked bored.
3. The principal is self-indulgent.	3. The principal told many stories about his own experiences.

When I make an observation, I give someone the chance to respond. When I make an evaluation, I make a judgment. When we make a judgment, we are speaking heartlessly, and so create distance from the person we are speaking with. This is moralistic judgment.

Moralistic Judgment makes us use words that are caught up in what is right and wrong, which categorizes someone and splits the person from their action, and we become concerned with who is good, bad, normal, abnormal, intelligent, ignorant, and so on. If someone has done something wrong, then we judge them as a bad person.

Before I was an adult, I used words that did not reveal my inner thoughts and feelings. In other words, I communicated in a detached style. For instance, if my boss gave me a task that I did not want to do, I would label them as "unfair" or "nasty". This kind of communication involves judgment, and there are other kinds: blame, criticism, comparison, diagnoses, and insults are all forms of judgment.

When our focus is on evaluating, rather than acknowledging our own and another's needs, and how they can be met, we are like the security guards who do not notice that the worker is stealing wheelbarrows. For instance, if my partner wants more affection from me than I am giving, she may describe me as "clingy and dependent". If I am giving her more affection than she needs, I may be labeled as "pining and desperate".

Emotions

According to psychoanalyst Rollo May, a mature individual is capable of distinguishing their emotions into numerous variations, ranging from intense and passionate to subtle and sensitive, similar to the varying passages of a symphony. However, for most of us, our emotions are limited and basic, similar to the limited notes in a bugle call, as May would put it.

The English language often creates common confusion about the use of the word "feel" without actually expressing a feeling. An example would be "I feel that I was not welcomed," the words "I feel" should be replaced with "I think." Generally, feelings are not clearly expressed when the word "feeling" is followed by:

a) "that, like, as if":

- "I feel *that* you should be clearer."

- "I feel *like* a loser."

- "I feel *as if* I'm skating on thin ice."

b) "I, you, he, she, they, it":

- "I feel I am constantly on edge."

- "I feel it is impractical."

c) proper nouns and names:

- "I feel Amy has been manipulative."

- "I feel my boss is irresponsible."

At the same time, we don't need the word "feel" to express what it is we are feeling. We can simply say, "I'm hopeful" rather than "I'm feeling hopeful".

Sometimes, we use words that describe a kind of self-assessment, rather than words that convey genuine emotions. The following examples illustrate the difference:

Self-Evaluation	Genuine Emotion
I feel inadequate as a meditator. (This statement is an evaluation of my ability as a meditator, it does not express my emotions.)	- I feel *disappointed* in myself as a meditator. - I feel *impatient* as a meditator. - I feel *frustrated* when I meditate.
The key difference between the two is that one is an evaluation and the other is an observation.	

It also helps to distinguish between words that describe an action and those that express our emotions. The following may seem like expressions of emotion, but are actually assumptions about another's behavior.

Other-Evaluation	Genuine Emotion
I feel unimportant to my colleagues at work. (This	- I feel *sad* in the workplace.

statement is an evaluation of how other people perceive me, it does not express my emotions.)	- I feel *unheard* at work. - I feel *frustrated* when no one listens to me at work.
The key difference between the two is the same as the first example: one is an evaluation and the other is an observation.	

What is important about our emotions is that they move us, and so it is necessary to identify which emotions move us.

We might feel guilty, fearful, or ashamed when we respond to the values of others. This leads to our eventual downfall. The action itself will not foster goodwill from having to comply with internal or external pressure. It is likely to lead to resentment in the future, and a decrease in someone's self-esteem when they respond out of guilt, shame, or fear. Additionally, each time we respond to these feelings, we may associate someone with those feelings, and the likelihood of us responding to their needs with compassion is diminished.

It helps to have words with which to express ourselves, and below I have included some basic vocabulary lists. For example, we might say "That made me feel good", and the term "good" implies a number of things, like excitement, joy, happiness, or enthusiasm. Knowing these words will help us mature, as Rollo May suggests, because we will be better able to express our emotions and values.

These are words we can say when we feel like our values are being responded to:

absorbed	energetic	merry
adventurous	engrossed	mirthful
affectionate	enlivened	moved
alert	enthusiastic	optimistic
alive	excited	overjoyed
amazed	exhilarated	overwhelmed
amused	expansive	peaceful
animated	expectant	perky
appreciative	exultant	pleasant
ardent	fascinated	pleased
aroused	free	proud
astonished	friendly	quiet
blissful	fulfilled	radiant
breathless	glad	rapturous
buoyant	gleeful	refreshed
calm	glorious	relaxed
carefree	glowing	relieved
cheerful	good-humored	satisfied
comfortable	grateful	secure
complacent	gratified	sensitive
composed	happy	serene
concerned	helpful	spellbound
confident	hopeful	splendid
contented	inquisitive	stimulated
cool	inspired	surprised

curious	intense	tender
dazzled	interested	thankful
delighted	intrigued	thrilled
eager	invigorated	touched
ebullient	involved	tranquil
ecstatic	joyous, joyful	trusting
effervescent	jubilant	upbeat
elated	keyed-up	warm
enchanted	loving	wide-awake
encouraged	mellow	wonderful
		zestful

What we are likely to feel when someone ignores our values:

afraid	disgusted	intense
aggravated	disheartened	irate
agitated	dismayed	irked
alarmed	displeased	irritated
aloof	disquieted	jealous
angry	distressed	jittery
anguished	disturbed	keyed-up
annoyed	downcast	lazy
anxious	downhearted	leery
apathetic	dull	lethargic
apprehensive	edgy	listless
aroused	embarrassed	lonely
ashamed	embittered	mad

beat	exasperated	mean
bewildered	exhausted	miserable
bitter	fatigued	mopey
blah	fearful	morose
blue	fidgety	mournful
bored	forlorn	nervous
brokenhearted	frightened	nettled
chagrined	frustrated	numb
cold	furious	overwhelmed
concerned	gloomy	panicky
confused	guilty	passive
cool	harried	perplexed
cross	heavy	pessimistic
dejected	helpless	puzzled
depressed	hesitant	rancorous
despairing	horrified	reluctant
despondent	horrible	repelled
detached	hostile	resentful
disaffected	hot	restless
disenchanted	humdrum	sad
disappointed	hurt	scared
discouraged	impatient	sensitive
disgruntled	indifferent	shaky

Values

Expressions of judgments, criticisms, diagnoses, and interpretations of others are actually manifestations of our own values. When someone says, "You never understand me," they are expressing their unfulfilled value. Similarly, when a spouse claims "You've been working late every night this week; you love your work more than you love me," they are conveying that the value of intimacy has not been recognized.

However, when we indirectly express our values through evaluations, interpretations, and images, others may perceive it as criticism. In response to criticism, people often become defensive. To elicit a compassionate response, it is counterproductive to express our needs by interpreting or diagnosing someone else's behavior. Instead, we should explicitly connect our emotions to our values, so that others can respond with empathy.

Unfortunately, most of us have not been taught to think in terms of values. Instead, we tend to focus on others' faults when our needs are not being met. For instance, if we want our children to hang up their coats, we might label them as lazy for leaving them on the couch. Or, if our co-workers do not follow our preferred methods, we might consider them irresponsible by interpreting their actions.

On one occasion, I was tasked with mediating a dispute between migrant farmworkers and landowners. To initiate the mediation process, I inquired about the groups' requirements and any demands they may have had for the other party. However, instead of articulating their necessities, both groups were preoccupied with scrutinizing each other's alleged misdeeds. The farmworkers accused the landowners of racism, and the landowners accused the farmworkers of flouting the law. This demonstrated that both parties were more proficient at analyzing the perceived transgressions of the other group than expressing their own values clearly.

Time and again, I have observed that when people shift their focus from criticizing each other to discussing what they value, the likelihood of discovering solutions that accommodate everyone's values increases significantly. The subsequent values are some of the fundamental human values that we all possess.

Autonomy	Integrity
- To choose one's dreams, goals, and projects. - To choose the plan to fulfill those dreams, wishes, and desires.	- authenticity - creativity - meaning - self-worth
Celebration	**Interdependence**
- To celebrate the creation of life and dreams fulfilled. - To celebrate losses, loved ones, dreams (mourning).	- acceptance - appreciation - closeness - community - love - reassurance - support - trust - respect
Play	**Nurturance**
- laughter - fun	- food - rest - sexual expression - touch - health

The Pain of Unexpressed Values

Expressing one's values can be daunting in a world where people are often judged harshly for doing so. Women are particularly susceptible to this kind of criticism, as they have been socialized to view caregiving as their highest duty and to deny their own values to take care of others. This has led many women to ignore their own values, which can have detrimental effects. At a workshop, we discussed how internalizing these beliefs can lead to women asking for what they want in a way that reflects and reinforces the idea that they have no right to their values and that their values are unimportant. For example, instead of simply saying that she values some time to herself, a woman might make a case for it by listing all the things she did that day and imploringly asking if she can have some time for herself. This kind of weak argument can elicit resistance instead of compassion from others, making the speaker feel as if her values don't matter. It is important to learn how to express values in a clear and direct way so that they can be heard and valued by others.

Towards Emotional Liberation

As we progress towards emotional liberation, we tend to go through three stages in our relationship with others.

The first stage, also known as emotional slavery, is characterized by our belief that we are accountable for the emotions of those around us. We feel a constant need to ensure everyone is content, and if they are not, we feel obligated to fix it. This mindset can cause us to view our loved ones as a burden. Taking responsibility for the emotions of others can be harmful to our intimate relationships. I often hear people say, "I am afraid to be in a relationship," reflecting this sentiment.

It is common for people who view love as sacrificing their own needs to meet their partner's values, then feel overwhelmed and trapped when their partner is in pain or needs something. They may feel like they are in prison and need to escape the relationship quickly. Initially, in a new relationship, partners often relate to each other with joy and compassion, feeling a sense of freedom. However, as the relationship progresses and becomes more serious, partners may start to feel responsible for each other's emotions.

Stage 2 involves a realization of the negative consequences of constantly prioritizing the needs and feelings of others over one's own. This can lead to feelings of anger and a tendency to make comments such as "That's not my problem!" in response to others' pain. While we become clear about what we are not responsible for, we struggle to learn how to be responsible to others in a healthy way. Even after we begin to move away from emotional enslavement, we may still struggle with guilt and fear surrounding our own needs.

I recall an incident with my daughter, Anja, who had always prioritized the wishes of others over her own desires. When I encouraged her to express her needs more often, she protested, "I don't want to disappoint anybody, Dad!" I explained to her that being honest and expressing her needs would be a gift to others, and suggested ways for her to empathize with people without taking responsibility for their feelings.

Eventually, I saw evidence that Anja was becoming more comfortable expressing her needs. When her school principal scolded her for wearing overalls, Marla responded with a confident, "F____ off!" While she still had much to learn about respecting the needs of others while asserting her own, I celebrated this as a sign that she was moving away from emotional slavery and toward emotional liberation.

In the third stage, which is emotional liberation, our response to the needs of others comes from a place of compassion rather than fear, guilt, or shame. This leads to actions that are fulfilling not only for the recipients, but also for ourselves. We take full responsibility for our own intentions and actions but recognize that we are not responsible for the feelings of others. In this stage, we understand that meeting our own needs cannot come at the expense of others. We communicate our needs clearly, making it known that we also care about the fulfillment of others' needs.

An Exercise in Identifying Values

To practice identifying values, decide whether these statements communicate values or not by circling the number you believe the speaker is expressing their values.

1. "You irritate me when you leave company documents on the conference room floor."

2. "I feel angry when you say that, because I am wanting respect and I hear your words as an insult."

3. "I feel frustrated when you come late."

4. "I'm sad that you won't be coming for dinner because I was hoping we could spend the evening together."

5. "I feel disappointed because you said you would do it, and you didn't."

6. "I'm discouraged because I would have liked to have progressed further in my work by now."

7. "Little things people say sometimes hurt me."

8. "I feel happy that you received that award."

9. "I feel scared when you raise your voice."

10. "I am grateful that you offered me a ride because I needed to get home before my children."

Answers for the exercise:

1. The statement doesn't reveal the speaker's values but implies that the other person's behavior is solely responsible for the speaker's feelings. If the speaker was communicating their values, they could have said: "I want our documents to be easily accessible and safely stored, so I am irritated they were left on the floor."

2. The speaker is acknowledging responsibility for their feelings.

3. The speaker could have said, "I want to spend time with you, so I feel anxious when you cancel plans."

4. The speaker is acknowledging responsibility.

5. A better statement might be, "I want to feel heard and when you don't listen to me, I feel disrespected."

6. The speaker communicates their values.

7. An alternative could be, "I want to express myself, so I feel frustrated when you interrupt me."

8. See if this sounds better, "I value our time and so canceling plans last minute makes me feel disappointed."

9. Here's an example of expressing values, "I want to have a strong connection and when you ignore my messages I feel hurt."

10. Try this out instead, "I want to be treated with kindness and when you are sarcastic then I feel disrespected."

11. Yes, well said.

Chapter 5

THERAPY

This chapter introduces the therapies that Dr. Van der Kolk touched on in his book. These, however, require a professional.

Eye Movement Desensitization and Reprocessing (EMDR)

EMDR is a therapy that involves recalling traumatic memories while engaging in specific eye movements. It is a psychotherapy approach that was developed by Francine Shapiro in the late 1980s and involves a standardized eight-phase protocol that focuses on past memories, current triggers, and future potential challenges. The therapy also involves bilateral stimulation of the brain through eye movements, sounds, or taps to help process traumatic memories and promote healing.

A number of studies have shown the effectiveness of EMDR in treating PTSD and trauma-related symptoms. For example, a meta-analysis by Chen et al. (2014) found that EMDR was effective in reducing PTSD symptoms compared to waitlist or no treatment controls. Another meta-analysis by Bisson et al.

(2013) found that EMDR was just as effective as other trauma-focused therapies, such as cognitive-behavioral therapy (CBT).

Cognitive-Behavioral Therapy (CBT)

Cognitive-Behavioral Therapy (CBT) is a form of therapy that helps individuals identify and change negative thought patterns and behaviors related to their trauma. CBT is based on the idea that our thoughts, emotions, and behaviors are interconnected and that changing any one of these can lead to changes in the others.

Research has shown that CBT can be effective in treating a range of mental health conditions, including anxiety disorders, depression, and post-traumatic stress disorder (PTSD) (Hofmann, Asnaani, Vonk, Sawyer, & Fang, 2012; McEvoy, Nathan, & Norton, 2009; Sijbrandij et al., 2013).

In CBT, individuals work with a therapist to identify negative thought patterns and behaviors and learn new, more adaptive ways of thinking and responding to situations. This often involves learning and practicing specific skills, such as relaxation techniques and problem-solving strategies. CBT is typically short-term and structured, with sessions lasting 12-20 weeks.

Internal Family Systems Therapy (IFS)

Internal Family Systems Therapy (IFS) is a therapy that involves exploring and healing the various "parts" of the self that may have been affected by trauma. It focuses on identifying and addressing the various parts of an individual's personality that may be in conflict or causing distress. Through the process of identifying and communicating with these parts, individuals can learn to integrate them into a cohesive whole, resulting in increased self-awareness, self-compassion, and improved functioning.

Research on IFS therapy has been limited, but some studies have shown promising results. For example, a 2013 study found that IFS therapy was effective in reducing symptoms of post-traumatic stress disorder (PTSD) in a sample of women who had experienced childhood sexual abuse (Bozkurt et al., 2013). Another study from 2018 found that IFS therapy was effective in reducing symptoms of anxiety and depression in a sample of adults (Gantt & Tinnin, 2018).

Neurofeedback Therapy

Neurofeedback is a technique that uses real-time brainwave monitoring to help individuals learn to regulate their own brain activity. Neurofeedback therapy, also known as EEG biofeedback, is a type of therapy that involves training individuals to regulate their brain activity through visual or auditory feedback. According to a systematic review published in the Journal of Attention Disorders, neurofeedback therapy has shown promise in improving symptoms of attention-deficit/hyperactivity disorder (ADHD) and reducing medication use (Arns et al., 2014). Additionally, a meta-analysis published in the journal Applied Psychophysiology and Biofeedback found that neurofeedback therapy may be effective in reducing symptoms of anxiety and depression (Wang et al., 2019).

CONCLUSION

The goal of this book has been to translate science into practice, and we are on the cusp of embracing a trauma-informed approach.

Nobel Prize winner James Heckman demonstrated the immense savings produced by early intervention in the lives of children from poor and troubled families, resulting in more high school graduations, less criminality, increased employment, and decreased family and community violence. All over the world, there are people who take this data seriously and work tirelessly to develop and apply more effective interventions, including devoted teachers, social workers, doctors, therapists, nurses, philanthropists, theater directors, prison guards, police officers, and meditation coaches. If you've come this far in reading this book, you're also a part of this community.

Thanks to advances in neuroscience, we now have a better understanding of how trauma changes brain development, self-regulation, and our capacity to stay focused and connected with others. Sophisticated imaging techniques have identified the origins of PTSD in the brain, explaining why traumatized people become disengaged and sensitive to stimuli, and why they may react strongly to provocation. Understanding the fundamental processes that underlie traumatic stress opens the door to an array of interventions that can bring the brain areas related to self-regulation, self-perception, and attention back online. Chapters 1 and 2 dealt with these features of trauma.

As social beings, our brains are hardwired to facilitate collaboration and interaction. Trauma can shatter this social engagement system, hindering cooperation, nurturing, and the ability to function effectively in a group. The root cause of many mental health issues, such as drug addiction and self-harm, is often a lack of adequate human contact and support, which can make emotions unbearable. Institutions that work with traumatized individuals often overlook the emotional engagement system, which is essential to our well-being, and instead focus solely on correcting negative thinking and suppressing difficult emotions and behaviors. This was an important focus of Chapter 4.

Although conversations about post-traumatic stress disorder (PTSD) often center on soldiers returning from war or victims of terrorism and accidents, trauma is a much broader public health issue and could be the most significant threat to our well-being. Domestic violence alone has claimed more American lives since 2001 than the wars in Iraq and Afghanistan combined. Despite numerous campaigns to fund cancer research, there are no comparable efforts to address the fear, anger, and depression that follow trauma, which is a predictable consequence of experiencing trauma.

Our brains are inherently wired to facilitate social interaction and cooperation with others, as humans are fundamentally social beings. However, when trauma occurs, it can have a devastating impact on our social-engagement system, making it difficult to work together, nurture others, and contribute positively to our communities. Extensive research shows that many mental health issues, such as drug addiction and self-harm, stem from an inability to cope with overwhelming emotions due to a lack of social support. Unfortunately, institutions that aim to assist individuals affected by trauma often overlook the importance of emotional connection, instead prioritizing the correction of negative thought patterns and the suppression of difficult emotions and behaviors. This is why I spent much time discussing the role of art in Chapter 3.

As previously mentioned, relying solely on medication to manage conditions fails to address the underlying issues at hand. Instead, it's crucial to ask deeper questions about the patient's coping mechanisms and available resources. What internal or external tools do they have to manage stress and anxiety? Does someone have a healthy diet and exercise plan? Are they attuned to their bodies and working to build physical strength, vitality, and relaxation? Do they have healthy relationships with supportive individuals during challenging times? Are they active members of a community, contributing to the well-being of others? Additionally, identifying specific skills that may improve focus, decision-making, and attention, as well as helping them find purpose and recognize their unique strengths, is essential. Ultimately, the goal should be to empower patients to take control of their lives, rather than relying solely on medication to mask symptoms. When people feel secure and have positive relationships, they are less likely to resort to drugs, TV, or destructive behavior. They also avoid causing harm to themselves or others.

Encountering trauma exposes us to our own vulnerability and the cruelty that humans can inflict on each other. However, it also reveals our remarkable resilience. I have devoted my career to exploring the sources of joy, creativity, meaning, and connection that make life worth living, which has kept me going in this work for so long. Despite the immense suffering they have endured, many have gone on to become caring partners and parents, outstanding teachers, nurses, scientists, and artists.

Trauma is now one of our most pressing public health concerns, and we possess the knowledge necessary to respond effectively. The choice is ours to take action based on what we know. Now, with this workbook, the choices may be easier to choose again.

FAQS

Where do I start? What is a short-, medium-, and long-term plan?

Start immediately with exercise and diet. It will bring immediate results. Stick with that plan for at least three months. However, the easiest thing to start begin with Chapter 1. The results are the slowest but produce the most lasting changes. There is no need to do everything all at once, but long-term, one should be doing things that touch on all the chapters.

What are some examples of physical exercises that can be helpful for healing trauma, and how do they work?

Examples of physical exercises that can be helpful for healing trauma include yoga, dance, martial arts, and strength training. These exercises can help release tension and stress, increase body awareness, and promote a sense of empowerment and control over one's body.

How can I develop a regular mindfulness practice to help manage my trauma symptoms?

To develop a regular mindfulness practice, it can be helpful to start with short periods of meditation or other mindful activities such as mindful breathing, body scanning, or mindful walking. Consistency is key, so it's important to find a practice that works for you and make it a regular part of your routine.

What are some healthy eating habits that can support my overall well-being and healing from trauma?

Some healthy eating habits that can support overall well-being and healing from trauma include eating a balanced diet that includes whole foods, avoiding processed and sugary foods, staying hydrated, and avoiding alcohol and other substances that can interfere with emotional regulation.

How can artistic hobbies such as writing, drawing, or playing music be therapeutic for people who have experienced trauma?

Artistic hobbies such as writing, drawing, or playing music can be therapeutic for people who have experienced trauma because they can provide a creative outlet for emotions, help foster a sense of self-expression, and promote relaxation and mindfulness.

How can communication exercises such as active listening and assertive communication help me build healthier relationships?

Communication exercises such as active listening and assertive communication can help individuals build healthier relationships by improving communication skills and increasing empathy and understanding between individuals.

How can I find the motivation to continue practicing these healing techniques, especially when I feel discouraged or overwhelmed?

Finding motivation to continue practicing healing techniques can be challenging, but it can be helpful to set achievable goals, celebrate small victories, and remind oneself of the benefits of continued practice.

What are some potential challenges I might face while working through this workbook, and how can I prepare for them?

Potential challenges while working through the workbook may include feeling overwhelmed, struggling to engage in certain exercises, or facing difficult emotions or memories. To prepare, it may be helpful to seek support from a therapist or trusted individual, work at a pace that feels manageable, and practice self-compassion and self-care.

How can I adapt the exercises in this workbook to fit my individual needs and experiences with trauma?

Adapting exercises in the workbook to fit individual needs and experiences with trauma may involve modifying certain exercises or seeking support from a therapist or other mental health professional.

What are some potential benefits of completing this workbook, and how can I measure my progress and growth?

Potential benefits of completing the workbook may include increased self-awareness, improved coping skills, reduced trauma symptoms, and an overall sense of empowerment and healing.

How can I stay connected to a supportive community while working through this workbook?

Staying connected to a supportive community while working through the workbook can involve seeking out a support group, therapist, or online community of individuals who are also healing from trauma.

What are some potential limitations of using a workbook for healing from trauma, and how can I ensure that I am getting the support I need?

Potential limitations of using a workbook for healing from trauma include the need for additional support from a therapist or mental health professional, and the potential for certain exercises or techniques to trigger difficult emotions or memories.

How can I integrate the lessons and tools I have learned from this workbook into my daily life and continue to grow and heal over time?

Integrating the lessons and tools learned from the workbook into daily life can involve practicing self-care, seeking support when needed, and continuing to engage in practices that promote overall well-being and healing. It's important to remember that healing is an ongoing process and to celebrate progress along the way.

AUTHOR BIO

Dr. Kael Lifeson has a PhD in psychotherapy with many years of experience in helping patients overcome trauma and mental health problems. Specialized in motivation, personal growth, and trauma care, Dr. Lifeson has extensive knowledge of cognitive and behavioral therapy techniques and applies them regularly in his treatments.

Thanks to his extensive training in psychology and his passion for personal growth, Dr. Lifeson has gained a deep understanding of the challenges we face in life and how we can overcome them. His patient-centered approach and human warmth have made him one of the most valued therapists in his community.

In addition, Dr. Lifeson decided to share his experience by writing books on motivation, personal growth, and trauma care. His books have been highly appreciated by readers due to their clear and accessible writing and their ability to inspire and motivate readers to overcome their difficulties.

"I want my patients and readers of my books to know that there is always a light at the end of the tunnel, even when it seems that all is lost. Motivation and personal growth are possible for anyone, and I want to share my message of hope with as many people as possible."

This is why Dr. Kael Lifeson decided to write books about motivation, personal growth, and the care of trauma.

REFERENCES

Arns, M., de Ridder, S., Strehl, U., Breteler, M., & Coenen, A. (2014). Efficacy of neurofeedback treatment in ADHD: The effects on inattention, impulsivity and hyperactivity: A meta-analysis. *Journal of Attention Disorders, 18*(5), 435-447. doi: 10.1177/1087054712460087

Bleakley, S. (2017). *Mindfulness and Surfing: Reflections for Saltwater Souls.* Leaping Hare Press.

Bisson, J., Roberts, N. P., Andrew, M., Cooper, R., & Lewis, C. (2013). Psychological therapies for chronic post-traumatic stress disorder (PTSD) in adults. *Cochrane Database of Systematic Reviews,* (12), CD003388. https://doi.org/10.1002/14651858.CD003388.pub4

Bozkurt, M., Rochelle, K., Pennington, M. L., & Gonzalez, J. M. (2013). Efficacy of Internal Family Systems Therapy in Treating Survivors of Childhood Sexual Abuse. *Journal of Marital and Family Therapy, 39*(3), 305–319. https://doi.org/10.1111/jmft.12011

Chen, Y. R., Hung, K. W., Tsai, J. C., Chu, H., Chung, M. H., & Chen, S. R. (2014). Efficacy of eye-movement desensitization and reprocessing for patients with posttraumatic-stress disorder: a meta-analysis of randomized controlled trials. *PloS one, 9*(8), e103676. https://doi.org/10.1371/journal.pone.0103676

Darwin, C. (1998). *The Expression of the Emotions in Man and Animals*. Oxford University Press. (Original work published in 1872).

Gantt, L., & Tinnin, L. W. (2018). Internal Family Systems Therapy for Generalized Anxiety Disorder. *Journal of Contemporary Psychotherapy, 48*(1), 11–17. https://doi.org/10.1007/s10879-017-9362-4

Harvard Health Publishing. (2020). How trauma can affect your eating habits. https://www.health.harvard.edu/blog/how-trauma-can-affect-your-eating-habits-2020112421359

Hillesum, E. (1983). *Etty: A diary 1941-1943*. K.A.D. Smelik-Gladstone & A. van der Wal (Eds.). William B. Eerdmans Publishing Company.

Hofmann, S. G., Asnaani, A., Vonk, I. J., Sawyer, A. T., & Fang, A. (2012). The efficacy of cognitive behavioral therapy: A review of meta-analyses. *Cognitive Therapy and Research, 36*(5), 427-440.

Merleau-Ponty, M. (2012). *Phenomenology of Perception*. Routledge. (Original work published in 1945).

McEvoy, P. M., Nathan, P., & Norton, P. J. (2009). Efficacy of transdiagnostic treatments: A review of published outcome studies and future research directions. *Journal of Cognitive Psychotherapy, 23*(1), 20-33.

National Center for PTSD. (2021). *PTSD and problems with alcohol use*. U.S. Department of Veterans Affairs. https://www.ptsd.va.gov/understand/related/problem_alcohol_use.asp

Shapiro, F. (2018). *Eye movement desensitization and reprocessing (EMDR) therapy: Basic principles, protocols, and procedures*. Guilford Publications.

Sijbrandij, M., Kunovski, I. Y., Cuijpers, P., & Kleiboer, A. (2013). Psychological treatment of posttraumatic stress disorder (PTSD) in adult refugees: A systematic review and meta-analysis. *European Journal of Psychotraumatology*, 4(1), 1-18.

Substance Abuse and Mental Health Services Administration. (2014). *TIP 57: Trauma-informed care in behavioral health services.* https://store.samhsa.gov/product/TIP-57-Trauma-Informed-Care-in-Behavioral-Health-Services/SMA14-4816

Van der Kolk, B. (2014). *The Body Keeps the Score: Brain, Mind, and Body in the Healing of Trauma.* Penguin Books.

Wang, S. Y., Lin, I. M., & Fan, S. Y. (2019). Efficacy of neurofeedback treatment for anxiety disorders: A systematic review and meta-analysis. Applied Psychophysiology and Biofeedback, 44(4), 255-266. doi: 10.1007/s10484-019-09452-7

Made in United States
Troutdale, OR
10/18/2023

13809913R00066